Living Through the Civil Rights Movement

Other Books in the Living Through the Cold War series:

LIVING THROUGH
THE COLD WAR

Living Through the Civil Rights Movement

Charles George, Book Editor

GREENHAVEN PRESS
An imprint of Thomson Gale, a part of The Thomson Corporation

THOMSON
™
GALE

Detroit • New York • San Francisco • New Haven, Conn. • Waterville, Maine • London

Christine Nasso, *Publisher*
Elizabeth Des Chenes, *Managing Editor*

© 2007 Thomson Gale, a part of The Thomson Corporation.

Thomson and Star logo are trademarks and Gale and Greenhaven Press are registered trademarks used herein under license.

For more information, contact:
Greenhaven Press
27500 Drake Rd.
Farmington Hills, MI 48331-3535
Or you can visit our Internet site at http://www.gale.com

Articles in Greenhaven Press anthologies are often edited for length to meet page require-ments. In addition, original titles of these works are changed to clearly present the main thesis and to explicitly indicate the author's opinion. Every effort is made to ensure that Greenhaven Press accurately reflects the original intent of the authors. Every effort has been made to trace the owners of copyrighted material.

Cover photograph reproduced by permission of Bettman/Corbis.

LIBRARY OF CONGRESS CATALOGING-IN-PUBLICATION DATA

Living Through the Civil Rights Movement / Charles George, book editor.
    p. cm. -- (Living through the Cold War)
    Includes bibliographical references and index.
    ISBN-13: 978-0-7377-2919-1 (hardcover : alk. paper)
    ISBN-10: 0-7377-2919-8 (hardcover : alk. paper)
    1. African Americans--Civil rights--History--20th century--Sources 2. Civil rights movements--United States--History--20th century--Sources 3. African American civil rights workers--History--20th century--Sources 4. Civil rights workers--United States--History--20th century--Sources 5. Politicians--United States--History--20th century--Sources 6. Racism--United States--History--20th century --Sources 7. United States--Race relations--History--20th century--Sources 8. Southern States--Race relations--History--20th century--Sources I. George, Charles,1949– II. Series.
    E185.61.L595 2007
    323.1196'073009045--dc22
                                                                                2006017184

Printed in the United States of America
10 9 8 7 6 5 4 3 2 1

Contents

Chapter 2: Statements by Leaders of the Movement

Chapter 3: Foot Soldiers in the Movement: Voices from the Front Lines

Foreword

At the midpoint of the Cold War, in early 1968, U.S. television viewers saw surprising reports from Vietnam, where American ground troops had been fighting since 1965. They learned that South Vietnamese Communist rebels, known as the Vietcong, had attacked unexpectedly throughout the country. At one point Vietcong insurgents engaged U.S. troops and officials in a firefight at the very center of U.S. power in Vietnam, the American embassy in South Vietnam's capital, Saigon. Meanwhile, thousands of soldiers and marines faced a concerted siege at Khe Sanh, an isolated base high in central Vietnam's mountains. Their adversary was not the Vietcong, but rather the regular North Vietnamese army.

Reporters and U.S. citizens quickly learned that these events constituted the Tet Offensive, a coordinated attack by Vietnamese Communists that occurred in late January, the period of Tet, Vietnam's new year. The American public was surprised by the Tet Offensive because they had been led to believe that the United States and its South Vietnamese allies were winning the war, that Vietcong forces were weak and dwindling, and that the massive buildup of American forces (there were some five hundred thousand U.S. troops in Vietnam by early 1968) ensured that the south would remain free of a Communist takeover. Since 1965, politicians, pundits, and generals had claimed that massive American intervention was justified and that the war was being won. On a publicity tour in November 1967 General William Westmoreland, the American commander in Vietnam, had assured officials and reporters that "the ranks of the Vietcong are thinning steadily" and that "we have reached a point where the end begins to come into view." President Lyndon B. Johnson's advisers, meanwhile, continually encouraged him to publicly emphasize "the light at the end of the tunnel."

Ordinary Americans had largely supported the troop buildup in Vietnam, believing the argument that the country was an important front in the Cold War, the global effort to stop the spread of communism that had begun in the late 1940s. Communist regimes already held power in nearby China, North Korea, and in northern Vietnam; it was deemed necessary to hold the line in the south not only to prevent communism from taking hold there but to prevent other nations from falling to communism throughout Asia. In 1965, polls showed that 80 percent of Americans believed that intervention in Vietnam was justified despite the fact that involvement in this fight would alter American life in numerous ways. For example, young men faced the possibility of being drafted and sent to fight—and possibly die—in a war thousands of miles away. As the war progressed, citizens watched more and more of their sons—both draftees and enlisted men—being returned to the United States in coffins (approximately fifty-eight thousand Americans died in Vietnam). Antiwar protests roiled college campuses and sometimes the streets of major cities. The material costs of the war threatened domestic political reforms and America's economic health, offering the continuing specter of rising taxes and shrinking services. Nevertheless, as long as the fight was succeeding, a majority of Americans could accept these risks and sacrifices.

Tet changed many minds, suggesting as it did that the war was not, in fact, going well. When CBS news anchor Walter Cronkite, who was known as "the most trusted man in America," suggested in his broadcast on the evening of February 27 that the Vietnam War might be unwinnable and could only end in a stalemate, many people wondered if he might be right and began to suspect that the positive reports from generals and politicians might have been misleading. It was a turning point in the battle for public opinion. Johnson reportedly said that Cronkite's expressions of doubt signaled the loss of mainstream America's support for the war. Indeed, after Tet more and more people joined Cronkite in wondering whether fighting this obscure enemy in an isolated country halfway around the world was worth the cost—whether it was a truly important front in the Cold War. They made their views known through demonstrations and opinion polls, and politicians were forced to respond. In a dramatic and unexpected turn of events, Johnson declined to run for reelection in 1968, stating that his involvement in the political campaign would detract from his efforts to negotiate a peace agreement with North Vietnam. His successor, Richard Nixon, won the election after promising to end the war.

The Tet Offensive and its consequences provide strong examples of how the Cold War touched the lives of ordinary Americans. Far from being an abstract geopolitical event, the Cold War, as Tet reveals, was an ever-present influence in the everyday life of the nation. Greenhaven Press's Living Through the Cold War series provides snapshots into the lives of ordinary people during the Cold War, as well as their reactions to its major events and developments. Each volume is organized around a particular event or distinct stage of the Cold War. Primary documents such as eyewitness accounts and speeches give firsthand insights into both ordinary peoples' experiences and leaders' decisions. Secondary sources provide factual information and place events within a larger global and historical context. Additional resources include a detailed introduction, a comprehensive chronology, and a thorough bibliography. Also included are an annotated table of contents and a detailed index to help the reader locate information quickly. With these features, the Living Through the Cold War series reveals the human dimension of the superpower rivalry that defined the globe during most of the latter half of the twentieth century.

Introduction

American society changed radically for black Americans during the cold war. The most dramatic changes came between 1954 and 1968 during the civil rights movement, due in part to the advent of television news coverage. Prior to television, activists had limited success informing the public about the plight of African Americans. Outside the Deep South, people had only vague ideas about the hardships southern blacks suffered every day. During the civil rights movement television coverage allowed people across the nation—and around the world—to feel they were experiencing the struggle of black people firsthand.

The Emancipation Proclamation of 1863 and the Thirteenth Amendment to the U. S. Constitution granted freedom to America's slaves. But freedom and equality are not the same. Subsequent amendments were passed to ensure equality, but white southern politicians found loopholes in those guarantees, systematically revoking blacks' newly won rights through state laws, local ordinances, economic pressures, and outright intimidation. Well into the 1960s blacks were excluded from mainstream American life in the South. Restaurants, hotels, public swimming pools, parks, department stores, churches, hospitals, and even cemeteries were strictly segregated. Blacks could not vote and were relegated to inferior schools—thus condemned to ignorance and second-class citizenship.

Early Efforts to Expose Racial Discrimination

In the early twentieth century northern black activists like Ida B. Wells-Barnett, W.E.B. Du Bois, and A. Philip Randolph fought racial discrimination, hoping to win support for legislation to correct the injustice. Through protest marches, articles in black newspapers and magazines, speeches to national organizations, court cases, and direct conversations with U.S. presidents, these activists tried to publicize the plight of black Americans. Although they made some gains, major reform would not come for decades.

Stories about the efforts of African American activists were reported in newspapers, but such coverage was usually limited in scope and was easily censored by local editors. The development of radio broadcasting expanded news coverage, but its range was also limited, and southern stations usually refused to carry any program dealing with race. Television changed everything. The late Peter Jennings, anchor of ABC's *World News Tonight*, reflected on the difference between television and other media in his book *The Century*:

> On radio, or in print, the issue of civil rights could be muted by the polite quality of words; in court decisions it could get waylaid in abstract constitutional arguments over states' rights. But on television the issue was made plain and simple through the power of images: while much of the nation watched, peaceful demonstrators asking for the most basic elements of respect were greeted with fire hoses and police dogs. The subtleties of the law mattered little here; on television, villains were villains and victims were victims.[1]

Television and the Movement Come of Age

Commercial television first appeared in the northeastern United States in the 1930s. By 1949 there were 1.6 million TV sets in the United States. Two years later there were 15 million. Into this rapidly expanding audience stepped legendary radio and television pioneer Edward R. Murrow. His CBS news program *See It Now* aired the first discussion of civil rights on May 18, 1954, when he interviewed southerners to gauge their reaction to the U. S. Supreme Court's ruling in *Brown v. Board of Education*, which abolished segregated schools. Murrow and his successors used what he called "a powerful focusing flashlight"[2] to shine the light of truth into dark corners of the segregated South.

By 1955, the year the Montgomery, Alabama, bus boycott began, 92 percent of American homes contained televisions, and viewers watched an average of five hours a day. At about the same time, NBC, CBS, and ABC expanded their nightly news shows to a half hour. Network executives, recognizing the drama and sensationalism of the civil rights struggle, sent camera crews and reporters to cover confrontations between protesters and police. The first incident involving violence occurred in 1957 in Little Rock, Arkansas. Television cameras recorded an angry segregationist mob cursing and yelling, attacking black reporters, and trying to prevent nine black students from entering Central High School.

In 1960 prime-time news programs such as NBC's *White Paper*, ABC's *Bell and Howell Close-Up*, and *CBS Reports*, joined the nightly news, covering every aspect of the civil rights struggle. *White Paper*'s hour-long "Nashville Sit-In" in 1959 showed black college students attempting to get service at segregated lunch counters in Nashville, Tennessee. Instead, the protesters received refusals from owners and abuse from white patrons. Viewers were equally appalled in 1961 at images of Freedom Riders being attacked in Alabama, when members of the Ku Klux Klan burned buses, threw rocks, and beat students.

Three later events—demonstrations in Birmingham, Alabama, the March on Washington, and the march in Selma, Alabama—are considered turning points in the civil rights struggle. In each instance, largely due to media-savvy civil rights leaders such as Martin Luther King Jr., television served to mold public opinion in favor of the civil rights movement and force Congress and the president to act.

Birmingham, Alabama

King knew the movement needed something drastic and dramatic to drive home its message in 1963. Birmingham, considered the most segregated city in America, offered just that. The city's segregationist police chief, "Bull" Connor, had a notoriously bad temper. King knew that pushed hard enough, Connor would probably respond with violence and expose in vivid detail the differences between nonviolent demonstrators, many of them schoolchildren protesting for basic rights, and hostile policemen bent on denying them those rights. In other words, the situation could produce great images for TV.

In Birmingham the strategy was to overwhelm the judicial system, fill the jails with marchers, and overload the courts. King hoped that this effort would force Connor to use extreme measures to stop marchers rather than arrest them. That happened on Friday, May 3, 1963, when Connor ordered his officers to use police dogs and high-pressure fire hoses on the marchers. One historian, Stewart Burns, then a high school student in Massachusetts, recalls what he saw on television that day:

> The sight and sound of this water massacre—tiny girls screaming, shirts torn off boys, soaked children piled on each other—left an indelible memory on millions of television viewers, including this writer. . . . Television that had first shown its pizzazz with Elvis Presley in 1956 and its ability to anoint presidents with the 1960 Kennedy-Nixon debates now showed its power to make history in the streets.[3]

The March on Washington

A few months later the movement turned its attention to the streets of Washington, D.C. Nearly a quarter of a million people gathered peacefully in front of the Lincoln Memorial. More TV cameras were there to record the spectacle than for any previous event. The March on Washington was the crowning event of the civil rights movement and brought Martin Luther King Jr. and his dream for America into more homes than ever before.

The march, featuring King's "I Have a Dream" speech, was also one of the first events to be broadcast live, via satellite, around the world. King's impassioned vision of a color-blind America touched millions of viewers across the globe. For many, it was the first opportunity to witness King's charismatic presence and eloquent oratory skills. It was also the first time that many people around the world had a chance to appreciate the grievances and goals of the civil rights movement.

Selma

One year later, in 1964, world attention was drawn to Selma, Alabama. On Sunday, March 7, about six hundred people marched across Selma's Edmund Pettus Bridge in protest of the state's voting restrictions. As they reached the other side, Selma's quick-tempered sheriff, Jim Clark, ordered his officers to attack the marchers. Though television cameras were pushed far back from the action, telephoto lenses captured the scene.

Filmed images of "Bloody Sunday" had an almost surreal quality. When ABC interrupted its prime-time movie *Judgment at Nuremberg*, a story about Nazi war crimes trials, to show film from Selma, many viewers thought they were witnessing newsreel images from Nazi concentration camps. The televised images had an immediate impact across the country. One of those watching, George B. Leonard from San Francisco, later wrote about the experience:

> A shrill cry of terror, unlike any sound that had passed through a TV set, rose up as the troopers lumbered forward, stumbling on fallen bodies. The scene cut to charging horses, their hoofs flashing over the fallen. Another quick cut: a cloud of tear gas billowed over the highway. Periodically the top of a helmeted head emerged from the cloud, followed by a club on the upswing. The club and the head would disappear into the cloud of gas and another club would bob up and down. *Unhuman.* No other word can describe the motions.[4]

The next morning Leonard and thousands of others were on their way to Alabama to stand alongside the demonstrators.

One week later President Lyndon Johnson, horrified by what had happened there to American citizens merely trying to register to vote, addressed Congress and the nation and demanded action. John Lewis, then leader of the Selma march and a member of Congress since 1986, said, "If it hadn't been for television on that day, we wouldn't have gotten the Voting Rights Act of 1965. The Civil Rights Movement in this country owes a great deal to television."[5] Without it, the nation's conscience might never have been stirred.

Notes

1. Peter Jennings and Todd Brewster, *The Century*. New York: Bantam Doubleday Dell, 1998, pp. 352–54.
2. Quoted in Alexander Kendrick, *Prime Time: The Life of Edward R. Murrow*. Boston: Little, Brown, 1969, p. 3.
3. Stewart Burns, *To the Mountaintop: Martin Luther King Jr.'s Sacred Mission to Save America, 1955–1968*. New York: HarperCollins, 2004, pp. 192–93.
4. Quoted in Clayborne Carson et al., eds., *The Eyes on the Prize Civil Rights Reader: Documents, Speeches, and Firsthand Accounts from the Black Freedom Struggle, 1954–1990*. New York: Penguin, 1991, pp. 213–14.
5. Quoted in Rodger Streitmatter, *Mightier than the Sword: How the News Media Have Shaped American History*. Boulder, CO: Westview, 1997, p. 186.

CHAPTER 1

LIVING THROUGH
THE COLD WAR

Government Officials
Speak Out

Responding to the School Integration Crisis in Little Rock

Dwight D. Eisenhower

In late summer 1957 the local school board of Little Rock, Arkansas, was prepared to implement a plan to begin integrating its schools. Most local citizens, though not altogether happy about the situation, agreed to the plan. Arkansas's governor, Orval Faubus, however, made Little Rock the scene of the first nationally telecast civil rights confrontation when he ordered members of the state militia to prevent black students from entering Central High School. A federal judge ordered the troops removed, but angry mobs of whites, most from outside Little Rock, surrounded the school, making desegregation impossible.

Faced with this difficult situation, Dwight D. Eisenhower, the thirty-fourth president of the United States, reluctantly ordered federal troops to surround the school to restore order and to see that the federal courts' rulings were obeyed. On the evening of September 24, 1957, he addressed the nation from the Oval Office. In his speech he explained the situation in Arkansas, discussed the philosophical basis of America's rule of law, and made clear why he could not allow mob rule in the streets of any American city. His speech was broadcast live on national television.

For a few minutes this evening I want to speak to you about the serious situation that has arisen in Little Rock. To make this talk I have come to the President's office in the White House. I could have spoken from Rhode Island, where I have been staying recently; but I felt that, in speaking from

Dwight D. Eisenhower, *Public Papers of the Presidents of the United States: Dwight D. Eisenhower.* Washington, D.C.: Federal Register Division, National Archives and Records Service, 1957.

the house of Lincoln, of Jackson, and of Wilson, my words would better convey both the sadness I feel in the action I was compelled today to take and the firmness with which I intend to pursue this course until the orders of the federal court at Little Rock can be executed without unlawful interference.

In that city, under the leadership of demagogic extremists, disorderly mobs have deliberately prevented the carrying out of proper orders from a federal court. Local authorities have not eliminated that violent opposition, and, under the law, I yesterday issued a proclamation calling upon the mob to disperse. This morning the mob again gathered in front of the Central High School of Little Rock, obviously for the purpose of again preventing the carrying out of the court's order relating to the admission of Negro children to that school.

Presidential Action Required

Whenever normal agencies prove inadequate to the task and it becomes necessary for the executive branch of the federal government to use its powers and authority to uphold federal courts, the President's responsibility is inescapable. In accordance with that responsibility, I have today issued an executive order directing the use of troops under federal authority to aid in the execution of federal law at Little Rock, Arkansas. This became necessary when my proclamation of yesterday was not observed, and the obstruction of justice still continues.

It is important that the reasons for my action be understood by all our citizens.

As you know, the Supreme Court of the United States has decided that separate public educational facilities for the races are inherently unequal, and, therefore, compulsory school segregation laws are unconstitutional. Our personal opinions about the decision have no bearing on the matter of enforcement; the responsibility and authority of the Supreme Court to interpret the Constitution are very clear. Local federal courts were instructed by the Supreme Court to issue such orders and decrees as might be necessary to achieve admission to public schools without regard to race—and with all deliberate speed.

During the past several years, many communities in our Southern states have instituted public-school plans for gradual progress in the enrollment and attendance of school children of all races in order to bring themselves into compliance with the law of the land. They thus demonstrated to the world that we are a nation in which laws, not men, are supreme. I regret to say that this truth—the cornerstone of our liberties—was not observed in this instance.

It was my hope that this localized situation would be brought under control by city and state authorities. If the use of local police powers had been sufficient, our traditional method of leaving the problems in those hands would have been pursued. But when large gatherings of obstructionists made it impossible for the decrees of the court to be carried out, both the law and the national interest demanded that the President take action.

The Situation in Little Rock

Here is the sequence of events in the development of the Little Rock school case.

In May of 1955, the Little Rock School Board approved a moderate plan for the gradual desegregation of the public schools in that city. It provided that a start toward integration would be made at the present term in high school, and that the plan would be in full operation by 1963. Here I might say that, in a number of communities in Arkansas, integration in the schools has already started and without violence of any kind. Now, this Little Rock plan was challenged in the courts by some who believed that the period of time as proposed in the plan was too long.

The United States court at Little Rock, which has supervisory responsibility under the law for the plan of desegregation in the public schools, dismissed the challenge, thus approving a gradual rather than an abrupt change from the existing system. The court found that the School Board had acted in good faith in planning for a public-school system free from racial discrimination. Since that time, the court has, on three separate occasions, issued orders directing that the plan be carried out. All persons were instructed to refrain from interfering with the efforts of the School Board to comply with the law.

Proper and sensible observance of the law then demanded the respectful obedience which the nation has a right to expect from all its people. This, unfortunately, has not been the case at Little Rock. Certain misguided persons, many of them imported into Little Rock by agitators, have insisted upon defying the law and have sought to bring it into disrepute. The orders of the court have thus been frustrated.

Why Federal Troops?

The very basis of our individual rights and freedoms rests upon the certainty than the President and the executive branch of government will support and insure the carrying out of the decisions of the federal courts, even, when necessary, with all the means at the President's command. Unless the President did so, anarchy would result. There would be no security for any except that which each one of us could provide for himself. The interest of the nation in the proper fulfillment of the law's requirements cannot yield to opposition and demonstrations by some few persons. Mob rule cannot be allowed to override the decisions of our courts.

Now, let me make it very clear that federal troops are not being used to relieve local and state authorities of their primary duty to preserve the peace and order of the community. Nor are the troops there for the purpose of taking over the responsibility of the School Board and the other responsible local officials in running Central High School. The running of our school system and the maintenance of peace and order in each of our states are strictly local affairs, and the federal government does not interfere except in a very few special cases and when requested by one of the several states. In the present case, the troops are there, pursuant to law, solely for the purpose of preventing interference with the orders of the court.

The proper use of the powers of the executive branch to enforce the orders of a federal court is limited to extraordinary and compelling circumstances. Manifestly, such an extreme situation has been created in Little Rock. This challenge must be met and with such measures as will preserve to the people as a whole their lawfully protected rights in a climate permitting their free and fair exercise.

Respect for the Law

The overwhelming majority of our people in every section of the country are united in their respect for observance of the law—even in those cases where they may disagree with that law. They deplore the call of extremists to violence.

The decision of the Supreme Court concerning school integration, of course, affects the South more seriously than it does other sections of the country. In that region I have many warm friends, some of them in the city of Little Rock. I have deemed it a great personal privilege to spend in our Southland tours of duty while in the military service and enjoyable recreational periods since that time. So, from intimate personal knowledge, I know that the overwhelming majority of the people in the South—including those of Arkansas and of Little Rock—are of goodwill, united in their efforts to preserve and respect the law even when they disagree with it. They do not sympathize with mob rule. They, like the rest of our nation, have proved in two great wars their readiness to sacrifice for America.

A foundation of our American way of life is our national respect for law. In the South, as elsewhere, citizens are keenly aware of the tremendous disservice that has been done to the people of Arkansas in the eyes of the nation, and that has been done to the nation in the eyes of the world.

Harm to the Nation

At a time when we face grave situations abroad because of the hatred that Communism bears toward a system of government based on human rights, it would be difficult to exaggerate the harm that is being done to the prestige and influence, and indeed to the safety, of our nation and the world. Our enemies are gloating over this incident and using it everywhere to misrepresent our whole nation. We are portrayed as a violator of those standards of conduct which the peoples of the world united to proclaim in the Charter of the United Nations. There they affirmed "faith in fundamental human rights" and "in the dignity and worth of the human person" and they did so "without distinction as to race, sex, language or religion."

And so, with deep confidence, I call upon the citizens of the state of Arkansas to assist in bringing to an immediate end all interference with the law and its processes. If resistance to the federal court orders ceases at once, the further presence of federal troops will be unnecessary, and the city of Little Rock will return to its normal habits of peace and order, and a blot upon the fair name and high honor of our nation in the world will be removed.

Thus will be restored the image of America and of all its parts as one nation, indivisible, with liberty and justice for all.

The Nation Faces a Moral Crisis in Regard to Race

John F. Kennedy

In 1963 the civil rights movement moved into Birmingham, Alabama, which Martin Luther King Jr. described as the most segregated city in America. Demonstrations were met with snarling police dogs and high-pressure fire hoses, and television coverage of the violence shocked the nation. A short while later, Alabama governor George C. Wallace stood in the doorway of the University of Alabama, refusing to obey a federal court order to allow its integration.

Faced with increasing violence and open rebellion in some southern states, John F. Kennedy, the thirty-fifth president of the United States, addressed the American people about the country's worsening race problem. In a speech delivered on June 11, 1963, he told the nation that racial discrimination and injustice were a moral evil and a national disgrace that had to be confronted and eliminated. In eloquent language, Kennedy described the treatment African Americans faced and appealed to white Americans to imagine what they would do in the same situation.

Kennedy also declared his support for far-reaching civil rights legislation, but he did not live to see its passage. He was assassinated on November 22, five months after delivering this speech. The legislation he describes in the speech was passed and signed into law by the next president, Lyndon B. Johnson, in 1964.

Good evening, my fellow citizens. This afternoon, following a series of threats and defiant statements, the presence of Alabama National Guardsmen was required on the University of Alabama to carry out the final and unequivocal

John F. Kennedy, "Remarks of President Kennedy on Nationwide Radio and Television," *Congressional Records, Proceedings and Debates of the 88th Congress, First Session.* Washington, D.C.: National Archives and Records Service, 1963.

25

order of the U.S. District Court of the Northern District of Alabama. That order called for the admission of two clearly qualified young Alabama residents who happened to have been born Negro.

That they were admitted peacefully on the campus is due in good measure to the conduct of the students of the University of Alabama, who met their responsibilities in a constructive way.

I hope that every American, regardless of where he lives, will stop and examine his conscience about this and other related incidents. This Nation was founded by men of many nations and backgrounds. It was founded on the principle that all men are created equal, and that the rights of every man are diminished when the rights of one man are threatened.

Today we are committed to a worldwide struggle to promote and protect the rights of all who wish to be free, and when Americans are sent to Vietnam or West Berlin, we do not ask for whites only. It ought to be possible, therefore, for American students of any color to attend any public institution they select without having to be backed up by troops.

It ought to be possible for American consumers of any color to receive equal service in places of public accommodation, such as hotels and restaurants and theaters and retail stores, without being forced to resort to demonstrations in the street, and it ought to be possible for American citizens of any color to register and to vote in a free election without interference or fear of reprisal.

It ought to be possible, in short, for every American to enjoy the privileges of being American without regard to his race or his color. In short, every American ought to have the right to be treated as he would wish to be treated, as one would wish his children to be treated. But this is not the case.

What Blacks Must Face

The Negro baby born in America today, regardless of the section of the Nation in which he is born, has about one-half as much chance of completing high school as a white baby born in the same place on the same day, one-third as much chance of completing college, one-third as much chance of becoming a professional man, twice as much chance of becoming unemployed, about one-seventh as much chance of earning $10,000 a year, a life expectancy which is 7 years shorter, and the prospects of earning only half as much.

This is not a sectional issue. Difficulties over segregation and discrimination exist in every city, in every State of the Union, producing in many cities a rising tide of discontent that threatens the public safety. Nor is this a partisan issue in a time of domestic crisis. Men of good will and generosity should be able to unite regardless of party or politics. This is not even a legal or legislative issue alone. It is better to settle these matters in the courts than on the streets, and new laws are needed at every level, but law alone cannot make men see right.

We are confronted primarily with a moral issue. It is as old as the scriptures and is as clear as the American Constitution.

The heart of the question is whether all Americans are to be afforded equal rights and equal opportunities, whether we are going to treat our fellow Americans as we want to be treated. If an American, because his skin is dark, cannot eat lunch in a restaurant open to the public, if he cannot send his children to the best public school available, if he cannot vote for the public officials who represent him, if, in short, he cannot enjoy the full and free life which all of us want, then who among us would be content to have the color of his skin changed and stand in his place? Who among us would then be content with the counsels of patience and delay?

One hundred years of delay have passed since President Lincoln freed the slaves, yet their heirs, their grandsons, are not fully free. They are not yet freed from the bonds of injustice. They are not yet freed from social and economic oppression, and this Nation, for all its hopes and all its boasts, will not be fully free until all its citizens are free.

To show support for President John F. Kennedy's proposed civil rights bill, tens of thousands gather at the March for Jobs and Freedom in Washington, DC, August 28, 1963.
Library of Congress

We preach freedom around the world, and we mean it, and we cherish our freedom here at home, but are we to say to the world, and much more importantly, to each other that this is a land of the free except for the Negroes; that we have no second-class citizens except Negroes; that we have no class or caste system, no ghettoes, no master race except with respect to Negroes?

Now Is the Time to Act

Now the time has come for this Nation to fulfill its promise. The events in Birmingham and elsewhere have so increased the cries for equality that no city or State or legislative body can prudently choose to ignore them.

The fires of frustration and discord are burning in every city, North and South, where legal remedies are not at hand. Redress is sought in the streets, in demonstrations, parades and protests which create tensions and threaten violence and threaten lives.

We face, therefore, a moral crisis as a country and as a people. It cannot be met by repressive police action. It cannot be left to increased demonstrations in the streets. It cannot be quieted by token moves or talk. It is a time to act in the Congress, in your State and local legislative body and, above all, in all of our daily lives.

It is not enough to pin the blame on others, to say this is a problem of one section of the country or another, or deplore the fact that we face. A great change is at hand, and our task, our obligation, is to make that revolution, that change, peaceful and constructive for all.

Those who do nothing are inviting shame as well as violence. Those who act boldly are recognizing right as well as reality.

Next week I shall ask the Congress of the United States to act, to make a commitment it has not fully made in this century to the proposition that race has no place in American life or law. The Federal judiciary has upheld that proposition in a series of forthright cases. The executive branch has adopted that proposition in the conduct of its affairs, including the employment of Federal personnel, the use of Federal facilities, and the sale of federally financed housing.

But there are other necessary measures which only the Congress can provide, and they must be provided at this session. The old code of equity law under which we live commands for every wrong a remedy, but in too many communities, in too many parts of the country, wrongs are inflicted on

Negro citizens as there are no remedies at law. Unless the Congress acts, their only remedy is in the street.

I am therefore asking the Congress to enact legislation giving all Americans the right to be served in facilities which are open to the public—hotels, restaurants, theaters, retail stores, and similar establishments.

This seems to me to be an elementary right. Its denial is an arbitrary indignity that no American in 1963 should have to endure, but many do.

I have recently met with scores of business leaders urging them to take voluntary action to end this discrimination and I have been encouraged by their response, and in the last 2 weeks over 75 cities have seen progress made in desegregating these kinds of facilities. But many are unwilling to act alone, and for this reason, nationwide legislation is needed if we are to move this problem from the streets to the courts.

Enforcing School Integration

I am also asking Congress to authorize the Federal Government to participate more fully in lawsuits designed to end segregation in public education. We have succeeded in persuading many districts to desegregate voluntarily. Dozens have admitted Negroes without violence. Today a Negro is attending a State-supported institution in every one of our 50 States, but the pace is very slow.

Too many Negro children entering segregated grade schools at the time of the Supreme Court's decision 9 years ago will enter segregated high schools this fall, having suffered a loss which can never be restored. The lack of an adequate education denies the Negro a chance to get a decent job.

The orderly implementation of the Supreme Court decision, therefore, cannot be left solely to those who may not have the economic resources to carry [out] the legal action or who may be subject to harassment.

Other features will be also requested, including greater protection for the right to vote. But legislation, I repeat, cannot solve this problem alone. It must be solved in the homes of every American in every community across our country.

We Owe Ourselves a Better Country

In this respect, I want to pay tribute to those citizens North and South who have been working in their communities to make life better for all. They are acting not out of a sense of legal duty, but out of a sense of human decency.

Like our soldiers and sailors in all parts of the world, they are meeting freedom's challenge on the firing line, and I salute them for their honor and their courage.

My fellow Americans, this is a problem which faces us all—in every city of the North as well as the South. Today there are Negroes unemployed two or three times as many compared to whites, inadequate in education, moving into the large cities, unable to find work, young people particularly out of work without hope, denied equal rights, denied the opportunity to eat at a restaurant or lunch counter or go to a movie theater, denied the right to a decent education, denied almost today the right to attend a State university even though qualified. It seems to me that these are matters which concern us all, not merely Presidents or Congressmen or Governors, but every citizen of the United States.

This is one country. It has become one country because all of us and all the people who came here had an equal chance to develop their talents.

We cannot say to 10 percent of the population that you can't have that right; that your children can't have the chance to develop whatever talents they have; that the only way that they are going to get their rights is to go into the streets and demonstrate. I think we owe them and we owe ourselves a better country than that.

Therefore, I am asking for your help in making it easier for us to move ahead and to provide the kind of equality of treatment which we would want ourselves; to give a chance for every child to be educated to the limit of his talents.

As I have said before, not every child has an equal talent or an equal ability or an equal motivation, but they should have the equal right to develop their talent and their ability and their motivation to make something of themselves.

We have a right to expect that the Negro community will be responsible, will uphold the law, but they have a right to expect that the law will be fair; that the Constitution will be color blind, as Justice [John M.] Harlan said at the turn of the century.

This is what we are talking about and this is a matter which concerns this country and what it stands for, and in meeting it I ask the support of all of our citizens.

The Civil Rights Movement Threatens Individual and States' Rights

George C. Wallace

The Civil Rights Act of 1964, signed into law by President Lyndon B. Johnson on July 2, 1964, outlawed discrimination in voter registration, housing, hiring practices, and access to public facilities such as restaurants, hotels, motels, parks, theaters, and schools. Many Southerners believed that the legislation infringed on their constitutional rights by telling them whom they could associate with, live next door to, eat beside, and work with.

One Southerner who opposed the new law was Alabama's segregationist governor, George C. Wallace. He criticized the act in the following speech, delivered at the Southeastern Fairgrounds in Atlanta, Georgia, on July 4, 1964, during his campaign to become the Democratic nominee for U.S. president. He told voters that he felt the federal government violated the Constitution by dictating how states should operate their own public facilities— such as schools, parks, and transportation systems—and how they should run local elections. He also argued that the new law severely limited freedom of speech and freedom of association for individuals.

We come here today in deference to the memory of those stalwart patriots who on July 4, 1776, pledged their lives, their fortunes, and their sacred honor to establish and defend the proposition that governments are created by the people, empowered by the people, derive their just powers from the consent of the people, and must forever remain subservient to the will of the people.

George C. Wallace, "Speech: The Civil Rights Movement: Fraud, Sham, and Hoax, July 4, 1964," Alabama governor (1963–1967, Wallace), Speeches, 1961–1968, Alabama Department of Archives & History.

Today, 188 years later, we celebrate that occasion and find inspiration and determination and courage to preserve and protect the great principles of freedom enunciated in the Declaration of Independence.

It is therefore a cruel irony that the President of the United States has only yesterday signed into law the most monstrous piece of legislation ever enacted by the United States Congress.

It is a fraud, a sham, and a hoax.

Rights Destroyed by Congress

This bill will live in infamy. To sign it into law at any time is tragic. To do so upon the eve of the celebration of our independence insults the intelligence of the American people. It dishonors the memory of countless thousands of our dead who offered up their very lives in defense of principles which this bill destroys.

Never before in the history of this nation have so many human and property rights been destroyed by a single enactment of the Congress. It is an act of tyranny. It is the assassin's knife stuck in the back of liberty.

With this assassin's knife and a blackjack in the hand of the Federal force-cult, the left-wing liberals will try to force us back into bondage. Bondage to a tyranny more brutal than that imposed by the British monarchy which claimed power to rule over the lives of our forefathers under sanction of the Divine Right of kings.

Today, this tyranny is imposed by the central government which claims the right to rule over our lives under sanction of the omnipotent black-robed despots who sit on the bench of the United States Supreme Court.

This bill is fraudulent in intent, in design, and in execution.

It is misnamed. Each and every provision is mistitled. It was rammed through the Congress on the wave of ballyhoo, promotions, and publicity stunts reminiscent of [circus showman] P. T. Barnum.

It was enacted in an atmosphere of pressure, intimidation, and even cowardice, as demonstrated by the refusal of the United States Senate to adopt an amendment to submit the bill to a vote of the people.

The Bill Creates Federal Crimes

To illustrate the fraud—it is not a Civil Rights Bill. It is a Federal Penal Code. It creates Federal crimes which would take volumes to list and years to tabulate because it affects the lives of 192 million American citizens. Every person in every walk and station of life and every aspect of our daily lives becomes subject to the criminal provisions of this bill.

It threatens our freedom of speech, of assembly or association, and makes the exercise of these Freedoms a federal crime under certain conditions.

It affects our political rights, our right to trial by jury, our right to the full use and enjoyment of our private property, the freedom from search and seizure of our private property and possessions, the freedom from harassment by Federal police and, in short, all the rights of individuals inherent in a society of free men.

Ministers, lawyers, teachers, newspapers, and every private citizen must guard his speech and watch his actions to avoid the deliberately imposed booby traps put into this bill. It is designed to make Federal crimes of our customs, beliefs, and traditions. Therefore, under the fantastic powers of the Federal judiciary to punish for contempt of court and under their fantastic powers to regulate our most intimate aspects of our lives by injunction, every American citizen is in jeopardy and must stand guard against these despots. . . .

I Will Have Nothing to Do with It!

[Senator Hubert Humphrey suggested,] now that the Civil Rights Bill is passed, that the President call the fifty state Governors together to work out ways and means to enforce this rotten measure.

There is no need for him to call on me. I am not about to be a party to anything having to do with the law that is going to destroy individual freedom and liberty in this country.

I am having nothing to do with enforcing a law that will destroy our free enterprise system.

I am having nothing to do with enforcing a law that will destroy neighborhood schools.

I am having nothing to do with enforcing a law that will destroy the rights of private property.

I am having nothing to do with enforcing a law that destroys your right—and my right—to choose my neighbors—or to sell my house to whomever I choose.

I am having nothing to do with enforcing a law that destroys the labor seniority system.

I am having nothing to do with this so-called civil rights bill.

The liberal left-wingers have passed it. Now let them employ some pinknik [Communist sympathizer] social engineers in Washington, D.C., to figure out what to do with it. . . .

We Must Stand Up for Individual Rights

In our nation, man has always been sovereign and the state has been his servant. This philosophy has made the United States the greatest free nation in history. This freedom was not a gift. It was won by work, by sweat, by tears, by war, by whatever it took to be—and to remain free. Are we today less resolute, less determined and courageous than our fathers and our grandfathers? Are we to abandon this priceless heritage that has carried us to our present position of achievement and leadership? I say if we are to abandon our heritage, let it be done in the open and full knowledge of what we do.

We are not unmindful and careless of our future. We will not stand aside while our conscientious convictions tell us that a dictatorial Supreme Court has taken away our rights and our liberties. We will not stand idly by while the Supreme Court continues to invade the prerogatives left rightfully to the states by the constitution.

We must not be misled by left-wing incompetent news media that day after day feed us a diet of fantasy, telling us we are bigots, racists, and hate-mongers to oppose the destruction of the constitution and our nation.

A left-wing monster has risen up in this nation. It has invaded the government. It has invaded the news media. It has invaded the leadership of many of our churches. It has invaded every phase and aspect of the life of freedom-loving people. It consists of many and various and powerful interests, but it has combined into one massive drive and is held together by the cohesive power of the emotions, setting forth civil rights as supreme to all. But, in reality, it is a drive to destroy the rights of private property, to destroy the freedom and liberty of you and me. And, my friends, where there are no property rights, there are no human rights. Red China and Soviet Russia are prime examples.

Politically evil men have combined and arranged themselves against us. The good people of this nation must now associate themselves together, else we will fall one by one, an unpitied sacrifice in a struggle which threatens to engulf the entire nation.

Blacks Must Have the Right to Vote

Lyndon B. Johnson

In most Southern counties before 1965, discriminatory practices of white election officials—poll taxes, literacy tests, and other measures—prevented blacks from successfully registering to vote. On March 7 of that year a group of activists protested these violations by attempting to march from Selma, Alabama, to the state capitol in Montgomery. They were brutally attacked by state troopers and local deputies at the Edmund Pettus Bridge in Selma. The carnage, captured by photographers and television crews, sparked national outrage and spurred Lyndon B. Johnson, the thirty-sixth president of the United States, to call upon Congress for a new voting rights bill.

On the evening of March 15, 1965, in a nationally televised address, Johnson urged a joint session of Congress to enact strong legislation to eliminate the contrived obstacles African Americans faced in order to vote. In his televised message he appealed to all Americans to remember the assertion of their nation's founders that "all men are created equal." He pointed out that a citizen's right to vote is the most basic individual right and should never be denied. During his speech, which also discussed poverty, ignorance, and disease, Johnson graphically voiced his solidarity with the civil rights marchers by using the movement's own phrase, "We shall overcome."

Mr. Speaker [of the House], Mr. President [of the Senate], Members of the Congress, I speak tonight for the dignity of man and the destiny of democracy.

Lyndon B. Johnson, "President Johnson's Selma Speech," March 15, 1965. National Archives and Records.

I urge every member of both parties—Americans of all religions and of all colors—from every section of this country—to join me in that cause.

Cause for Hope

At times history and fate meet at a single time in a single place to shape a turning point in man's unending search for freedom. So it was at Lexington and Concord. So it was a century ago at Appomattox. So it was last week in Selma, Alabama.

There, long-suffering men and women peacefully protested the denial of their rights as Americans. Many were brutally assaulted. One good man [James Reeb]—a man of God—was killed.

There was no cause for pride in what has happened in Selma.

There is no cause for self-satisfaction in the long denial of equal rights of millions of Americans.

But there is cause for hope and for faith in our democracy in what is happening here tonight.

For the cries of pain, and the hymns and protests of oppressed people, have summoned into convocation all the majesty of this great Government, the Government of the greatest Nation on earth.

Our mission is at once the oldest and most basic of this country: to right wrong, to do justice, to serve man.

In our time we have come to live with the moments of great crisis. Our lives have been marked with debate about great issues—issues of war and peace, issues of prosperity and depression. But rarely, in any time, does an issue lay bare the secret heart of America itself. Rarely are we met with the challenge, not to our growth or abundance, or our welfare or our security—but rather to the values and the purposes and the meaning of our beloved Nation.

An American Problem

The issue of equal rights for American Negroes is such an issue. And should we defeat every enemy, and should we double our wealth and conquer the stars and still be unequal to this issue, then we will have failed as a people and as a nation.

For with a country as with a person, "What is a man profited, if he shall gain the whole world, and lose his own soul?"

There is no Negro problem. There is no southern problem. There is no northern problem. There is only an American problem.

And we are met here tonight as Americans—not as Democrats or Republicans—we are met here as Americans to solve that problem.

This was the first nation in the history of the world to be founded with a purpose. The great phrases of that purpose still sound in every American heart, north and south: "All men are created equal"—"Government by consent of the governed"—"Give me liberty or give me death." And those are not just clever words and those are not just empty theories. In their name Americans have fought and died for two centuries and tonight around the world they stand there as guardians of our liberty risking their lives.

Those words are a promise to every citizen that he shall share in the dignity of man. This dignity cannot be found in a man's possessions. It cannot be found in his power or in his position. It really rests on his right to be treated as a man equal in opportunity to all others. It says that he shall share in freedom, he shall choose his leaders, educate his children, provide for his family according to his ability and his merits as a human being.

To apply any other test—to deny a man his hopes because of his color or race or his religion or the place of his birth—is not only to do injustice, it is to deny America and to dishonor the dead who gave their lives for American freedom.

Voting Is the Most Basic Right

Our fathers believed that if this noble view of the rights of man was to flourish, it must be rooted in democracy. The most basic right of all was the right to choose your own leaders. The history of this country in large measure, is the history of the expansion of that right to all of our people.

Many of the issues of civil rights are very complex and most difficult. But about this there can and should be no argument. Every American citizen must have an equal right to vote. There is no reason which can excuse the denial of that right. There is no duty which weighs more heavily on us than the duty we have to insure that right.

Yet the harsh fact is that in many places in this country men and women are kept from voting simply because they are Negroes.

Every device of which human ingenuity is capable has been used to deny this right. The Negro citizen may go to register only to be told that the day is wrong, or the hour is late, or the official in charge is absent.

And if he persists, and if he manages to present himself to the registrar, he may be disqualified because he did not spell out his middle name or because he abbreviated a word on the application.

And if he manages to fill out an application he is given a test. The registrar is the sole judge of whether he passes this test. He may be asked to recite the entire Constitution, or explain the most complex provisions of State law and even a college degree cannot be used to prove that he can read and write.

For the fact is that the only way to pass these barriers is to show a white skin.

The Need for a Voting Rights Act

Experience has clearly shown that the existing process of law cannot overcome systematic and ingenious discrimination. No law that we now have on the books—and I have helped to put three of them there—can insure the right to vote when local officials are determined to deny it.

In such a case our duty must be clear to all of us. The Constitution says that no person shall be kept from voting because of his race or his color. We have all sworn an oath before God to support and to defend that Constitution.

We must now act in obedience to that oath.

Wednesday I will send to Congress a law designed to eliminate illegal barriers to the right to vote. . . .

This bill will strike down restrictions to voting in all elections—Federal, State, and local—which have been used to deny Negroes the right to vote.

This bill will establish a simple, uniform standard which cannot be abused however ingenious the effort to flout our Constitution.

It will provide for citizens to be registered by officials of the U.S. Government if the State officials refuse to register them.

It will eliminate tedious, unnecessary lawsuits which delay the right to vote.

Finally, this legislation will insure that properly registered individuals are not prohibited from voting.

I will welcome the suggestions from all the Members of Congress—I have no doubt that I will get some—on ways and means to strengthen this law and to make it effective. But experience has plainly shown that this is the only path to carry out the command of the Constitution.

A Call for Action

To those who seek to avoid action by their National Government in their home communities—who want to and who seek to maintain purely local control over elections—the answer is simple.

Open your polling places to all your people.

Allow men and women to register and vote whatever the color of their skin.

Extend the rights of citizenship to every citizen of this land.

There is no constitutional issue here. The command of the Constitution is plain.

There is no moral issue. It is wrong—deadly wrong—to deny any of your fellow Americans the right to vote in this country.

There is no issue of States rights or National rights. There is only the struggle for human rights.

I have not the slightest doubt what will be your answer. . . .

Their Cause Must Be Our Cause

But even if we pass this bill, the battle will not be over. What happened in Selma is part of a far larger movement which reaches into every section and State of America. It is the effort of American Negroes to secure for themselves the full blessings of American life.

Their cause must be our cause, too, because it is not just Negroes, but really it is all of us, who must overcome the crippling legacy of bigotry and injustice. And we shall overcome.

As a man whose roots go deeply into southern soil I know how agonizing racial feelings are. I know how difficult it is to reshape the attitudes and the structure of our society.

But a century has passed—more than 100 years—since the Negro was freed. And he is not fully free tonight. It was more than 100 years ago that Abraham Lincoln, a great President of another party, signed the Emancipation Proclamation. But emancipation is a proclamation and not a fact.

A century has passed—more than 100 years—since equality was promised. And yet the Negro is not equal. A century has passed since the day of promise. And the promise is unkept.

The time of justice has now come. And I tell you that I believe sincerely that no force can hold it back. It is right—in the eyes of man and God—that it should come. And when it does, I think that day will brighten the lives of every American.

For Negroes are not the only victims. How many white children have gone uneducated and how many white families have lived in stark poverty—how many white lives have been scarred by fear because we have wasted our energy and our substance to maintain the barriers of hatred and terror?

We Shall Overcome

And so I say to all of you here and to all in the Nation tonight that those who appeal to you to hold on to the past do so at the cost of denying you your future.

This great, rich, restless country can offer opportunity and education and hope to all—all black and white, all North and South, sharecropper and city dweller. These are the enemies—poverty, ignorance, disease—they are our enemies, not our fellow man, not our neighbor. And these enemies too—poverty, disease, and ignorance—we shall overcome.

Now let none of us, in any section, look with prideful righteousness on the troubles in another section or the problems of our neighbors. There is really no part of America where the promise of equality has been fully kept. In Buffalo as well as in Birmingham, in Philadelphia as well as Selma, Americans are struggling for the fruits of freedom.

This is one nation. What happens in Selma or in Cincinnati is a matter of legitimate concern to every American. But let us look within our own hearts and our own communities, and let each of us put our shoulder to the wheel to root out injustice wherever it exists.

As we meet here in this peaceful, historic Chamber tonight, men from the South, some of whom were at Iwo Jima, men from the North, who have carried Old Glory to far corners of the world and brought it back without a stain on it, men from the East and from the West, are all fighting together without regard to religion or color or region in Vietnam. Men from every region fought for us across the world 20 years ago [in World War II].

And now, in these common dangers and then common sacrifices, the South made its contribution of honor and gallantry no less than any other region of the Great Republic, and in some instances—a great many of them—more.

And I have not the slightest doubt that good men from everywhere in this country—from the Great Lakes to the Gulf of Mexico, from the Golden Gate to the harbors along the Atlantic—will rally now together in this cause to vindicate the freedom of all Americans. For all of us owe this duty, and I believe that all of us will respond to it.

Your President makes that request of every American.

Praise for Nonviolent Demonstrations

The real hero of this struggle is the American Negro. His actions and protests—his courage to risk safety, and even to risk his life—have awakened the conscience of this Nation. His demonstrations have been designed to call attention to injustice, designed to provoke change, designed to stir freedom. He has called upon us to make good the promise of America. And who among us can say that we would have made the same progress were it not for his persistent bravery and his faith in American democracy?

For at the real heart of battle for equality is a deep-seated belief in the democratic process. Equality depends not on the force of arms or tear gas, but depends upon the force of moral right—not on recourse to violence but on respect for law and order.

There have been many pressures upon your President— and there will be others as the days come and go—but I pledge you tonight that we intend to fight this battle where it should be fought, in the courts and in the Congress and in the hearts of men.

We must preserve the right of free speech and the right of free assembly. But the right of free speech does not carry with it, as has been said, the right to holler "fire" in a crowded theater. We must preserve the right to free assembly, but free assembly does not carry with it the right to block public thoroughfares to traffic.

We do have a right to protest and a right to march under conditions that do not infringe the constitutional rights of our neighbors. And I intend to protect all those rights as long as I am permitted to serve in this office.

We will guard against violence, knowing it strikes from our hands the very weapons with which we seek progress—obedience to law, and belief in American values.

In Selma, as elsewhere, we seek and pray for peace. We seek order. We seek unity.

But we will not accept the peace of stifled rights, or the order imposed by fear, or the unity that stifles protest. For peace cannot be purchased at the cost of liberty. . . .

Opening the "City of Hope"

The bill that I am presenting to you will be known as a civil rights bill. But, in a larger sense, most of the program I am recommending is a civil rights program. Its object is to open the city of hope to all people of all races.

Because all Americans just must have the right to vote. And we are going to give them that right.

All Americans must have the privileges of citizenship regardless of race. And they are going to have those privileges of citizenship regardless of race.

But I would like to caution you and remind you that to exercise these privileges takes much more than legal right. It requires a trained mind and a healthy body. It requires a decent home, and the chance to find a job, and the opportunity to escape from the clutches of poverty.

Of course people cannot contribute to the Nation if they are never taught to read or write, if their bodies are stunted from hunger, if their sickness goes untended, if their life is spent in hopeless poverty just drawing a welfare check.

So we want to open the gates to opportunity. But we are also going to give all our people—black and white—the help that they need to walk through those gates.

My first job after college was as a teacher in Cotulla, Tex., in a small Mexican-American school. Few of them could speak English and I could not speak much Spanish. My students were poor and they often came to class without breakfast— hungry. And they knew, even in their youth the pain of prejudice. They never seemed to know why people disliked them, but they knew it was so because I saw it in their eyes.

I often walked home late in the afternoon after the classes were finished wishing there was more that I could do. But all I knew was to teach them the little that I knew—hoping that it might help them against the hardships that lay ahead.

Somehow you never forget what poverty and hatred can do when you see its scars on the hopeful face of a young child.

I never thought then in 1928 that I would be standing here in 1965. It never even occurred to me in my fondest dreams that I might have the chance to help the sons and daughters of those students—and to help people like them all over this country.

But now I do have that chance and I will let you in on a secret—I mean to use it.

Let's Work Together

And I hope that you will use it with me.

This is the richest and most powerful country which ever occupied this globe. The might of past empires is little compared to ours.

But I do not want to be the President who built empires, or sought grandeur, or extended dominion.

I want to be the President who educated young children to the wonders of their world.

I want to be the President who helped to feed the hungry and to prepare them to be taxpayers instead of tax-eaters.

I want to be the President who helped the poor to find their own way and who protected the right of every citizen to vote in every election.

I want to be the President who helped to end hatred among his fellow men and who promoted love among the people of all races and all regions and all parties.

I want to be the President who helped to end war among the brothers of this earth. . . .

I come here to ask you to share this task with me and to share it with the people we both work for.

I want this to be the Congress—Republicans and Democrats alike—which did all these things for all these people.

Beyond this great Chamber—out yonder in the 50 States are the people we serve. Who can tell what deep and unspoken hopes are in their hearts tonight as they sit there and listen? We all can guess, from our own lives, how difficult they often find their own pursuit of happiness; how many problems each little family has. They look most of all to themselves for their future.

But I think that they also look to each of us.

Above the pyramid on the great seal of the United States it says in Latin, "God has favored our undertaking."

God will not favor everything that we do. It is rather our duty to divine His will. I cannot help but believe that He truly understands and that He really favors the undertaking that we begin here tonight.

LIVING THROUGH
THE COLD WAR

CHAPTER 2

Statements by Leaders
of the Movement

"I Have a Dream"

Martin Luther King Jr.

When Martin Luther King Jr. was ordained a minister in 1948, he could not have imagined what lay ahead. In 1955, only months after becoming pastor of the Dexter Avenue Baptist Church in Montgomery, Alabama, he became leader of the Montgomery bus boycott, the first major demonstration in the American civil rights movement. Building on the success of the boycott, King and others organized the Southern Christian Leadership Conference (SCLC) in 1960 and gained international prominence with successful demonstrations throughout the South.

On August 28, 1963, before an estimated crowd of a quarter of a million people attending the March on Washington for civil rights, King delivered what many regard as one of the most inspiring speeches of the twentieth century. In the speech, which was nationally televised into millions of homes, King reminded listeners that the promises of America were still denied to African Americans in much of the country. He urged those in the movement not to abandon nonviolence as a means of achieving their goals, despite calls for a more militant stance by such leaders as Malcolm X. In closing, he held listeners spellbound as he shared his vision of racial equality in America.

I am happy to join with you today in what will go down in history as the greatest demonstration for freedom in the history of our nation.

Five score years ago, a great American in whose symbolic shadow we stand today signed the Emancipation Proclamation. This momentous decree came as a great beacon light of hope to millions of Negro slaves who had been seared in the flames of withering injustice. It came as a joyous daybreak to end the long night of their captivity.

Broken Promises

But one hundred years later, the Negro still is not free. One hundred years later, the life of the Negro is still sadly crippled by the manacles of segregation and the chains of discrimination. One hundred years later, the Negro lives on a lonely island of poverty in the midst of a vast ocean of material prosperity. One hundred years later, the Negro is still languishing in the corners of American society and finds himself an exile in his own land.

So we have come here today to dramatize a shameful condition. In a sense we have come to our nation's capital to cash a check. When the architects of our republic wrote the magnificent words of the Constitution and the Declaration of Independence, they were signing a promissory note to which every American was to fall heir. This note was a promise that all men—yes, black men as well as white men—would be guaranteed the inalienable rights of life, liberty, and the pursuit of happiness.

It is obvious today that America has defaulted on this promissory note insofar as her citizens of color are concerned. Instead of honoring this sacred obligation, America has given the Negro people a bad check, a check which has come back marked "insufficient funds." But we refuse to believe that the bank of justice is bankrupt. We refuse to believe that there are insufficient funds in the great vaults of opportunity of this nation. So we have come to cash this check, a check that will give us upon demand the riches of freedom and the security of justice.

Now Is the Time to Act

We have also come to this hallowed spot to remind America of the fierce urgency of now. This is no time to engage in the

Dr. Martin Luther King, Jr. Library of Congress

luxury of cooling off or to take the tranquilizing drug of gradualism. Now is the time to make real the promises of democracy. Now it the time to rise from the dark and desolate valley of segregation to the sunlit path of racial justice. Now is the time to lift our nation from the quicksands of racial injustice to the solid rock of brotherhood. Now is the time to make justice a reality for all of God's children. It would be fatal for the nation to overlook the urgency of the moment. This sweltering summer of the Negro's legitimate discontent will not pass until there is an invigorating autumn of freedom and equality.

Nineteen sixty-three is not an end, but a beginning. And those who hope that the Negro needed to blow off steam and will now be content will have a rude awakening if the nation returns to business as usual. There will be neither rest nor tranquility in America until the Negro is granted his citizenship rights. The whirlwinds of revolt will continue to shake the foundations of our nation until the bright day of justice emerges.

Renewed Call for Nonviolence

But there is something that I must say to my people who stand on the warm threshold which leads into the palace of justice. In the process of gaining our rightful place we must not be guilty of wrongful deeds. Let us not seek to satisfy our thirst for freedom by drinking from the cup of bitterness and hatred. We must forever conduct our struggle on the high plane of dignity and discipline. We must not allow our creative protest to degenerate into physical violence. Again and again we must rise to the majestic heights of meeting physical force with soul force.

The marvelous new militancy which has engulfed the Negro community must not lead us to a distrust of all white people, for many of our white brothers, as evidenced by their presence here today, have come to realize that their destiny is tied up with our destiny. They have come to realize that their freedom is inextricably bound to our freedom. We cannot walk alone.

And as we walk, we must make the pledge that we shall always march ahead. We cannot turn back. There are those who are asking the devotees of civil rights, "When will you be satisfied?" We can never be satisfied as long as the Negro is the victim of the unspeakable horrors of police brutality. We can never be satisfied as long as our bodies, heavy with the fatigue of travel, cannot gain lodging in the motels of the highways and the hotels of the cities. We cannot be satisfied as long as a Negro in Mississippi cannot vote, and a Negro in New York believes he has nothing for which to vote. No, no, we are not satisfied, and we will not be satisfied until justice rolls down like waters and righteousness like a mighty stream.

I am not unmindful that some of you have come here out of great trials and tribulation. Some of you come fresh from narrow jail cells. Some of you have come from areas where your quest for freedom left you battered by the storms of persecution and staggered by the winds of police brutality. You have been the veterans of creative suffering. Continue to work with the faith that unearned suffering is redemptive. Go back to Mississippi. Go back to Alabama. Go back to South Carolina. Go back to Georgia. Go back to Louisiana. Go back to the slums and ghettos of our northern cities, knowing that somehow this situation can and will be changed. Let us not wallow in the valley of despair.

"I Have a Dream"

I say to you today my friends, even though we face the difficulties of today and tomorrow, I still have a dream. It is a dream deeply rooted in the American dream. I have a dream that one day this nation will rise up and live out the true meaning of its creed: "We hold these truths to be self-evident, that all men are created equal."

I have a dream that one day on the red hills of Georgia the sons of former slaves and the sons of former slaveowners will be able to sit down together at the table of brotherhood.

I have a dream that one day, even the state of Mississippi, a state sweltering with the heat of injustice, a state sweltering with the heat of oppression, will be transformed into an oasis of freedom and justice.

I have a dream that my four little children will one day live in a nation where they will not be judged by the color of their skin but by the content of their character. I have a dream today.

I have a dream that one day, down in Alabama, with its vicious racists, with its governor having his lips dripping with the words of interposition and nullification, that one day right down in Alabama, little black boys and black girls will be able to join hands with little white boys and white girls as sisters and brothers. I have a dream today.

I have a dream that one day every valley shall be exalted, every hill and mountain shall be made low, the rough places will be made plain and the crooked places will be made straight and the glory of the Lord shall be revealed and all flesh shall see it together.

Let Freedom Ring!

This is our hope. This is the faith that I go back to the South with. With this faith we will be able to hew out of the mountain of despair a stone of hope. With this faith we will be able to transform the jangling discords of our nation into a beautiful symphony of brotherhood. With this faith we will be able to work together, to pray together, to struggle together, to go to jail together, to stand up for freedom together, knowing that we will be free one day. This will be the day, this will be the day when all of God's children will be able to sing with new meaning, "My country 'tis of thee,/ sweet land of liberty,/ of thee I sing./ Land where my fathers died,/ land of the Pilgrims' pride,/ from every mountainside,/ let freedom ring!" And if America is to be a great nation, this must become true.

So let freedom ring from the prodigious hilltops of New Hampshire. Let freedom ring from the mighty mountains of New York. Let freedom ring from the heightening Alleghenies of Pennsylvania. Let freedom ring from the snowcapped Rockies of Colorado. Let freedom ring from the curvaceous slopes of California. But not only that, let freedom ring from Stone Mountain of Georgia. Let freedom ring from Lookout Mountain of Tennessee. Let freedom ring from every hill and molehill of Mississippi. From every mountainside, let freedom ring.

And when this happens, when we allow freedom to ring, when we let it ring from every village and every hamlet, from every state and every city, we will be able to speed up that day when all of God's children—black men and white men, Jews and Gentiles, Protestants and Catholics—will be able to join hands and sing in the words of the old Negro spiritual, "Free at last, free at last. Thank God Almighty, we are free at last."

Revolution Cannot Be Peaceful

Malcolm X

During the height of the civil rights movement in the 1950s and 1960s, not all blacks were united behind the ideas of Martin Luther King Jr., including the tactics of nonviolent protest and the goal of racial integration. A controversial alternative vision of blacks in America was expressed in the black nationalist speeches and statements by Malcolm X.

We want to have just an off-the-cuff chat between you and me, us. We want to talk right down to earth in a language that everybody here can easily understand. We all agree tonight, all of the speakers have agreed, that America has a very serious problem. Not only does America have a very serious problem, but our people have a very serious problem. America's problem is us. We're her problem. The only reason she has a problem is she doesn't want us here. And every time you look at yourself, be you black, brown, red or yellow, a so-called Negro, you represent a person who poses such a serious problem for America because you're not wanted. Once you face this as a fact, then you can start plotting a course that will make you appear intelligent, instead of unintelligent.

What you and I need to do is learn to forget our differences. When we come together, we don't come together as Baptists or Methodists. You don't catch hell because you're a Baptist, and you don't catch hell because you're a Methodist. You don't catch hell because you're a Methodist or Baptist, you don't catch hell because you're a Democrat or a Republi-

Malcolm X, "Speech: Message to the Grass Roots, November 10, 1963," in *Malcolm X Speaks*, edited by George Breitman. New York: Pathfinder Press, 1989. Copyright © 1965, 1989 by Betty Shabazz and Pathfinder Press. Reproduced by permission.

can, you don't catch hell because you're a Mason or an Elk, and you sure don't catch hell because you're an American; because if you were an American, you wouldn't catch hell. You catch hell because you're a black man. You catch hell, all of us catch hell, for the same reason.

So we're all black people, so-called Negroes, second-class citizens, ex-slaves. You're nothing but an ex-slave. You don't like to be told that. But what else are you? You are ex-slaves. You didn't come here on the "Mayflower." You came here on a slave ship. In chains, like a horse, or a cow, or a chicken. And you were brought here by the people who came here on the "Mayflower," you were brought here by the so-called Pilgrims, or Founding Fathers. They were the ones who brought you here. . . .

The Black Revolution

I would like to make a few comments concerning the difference between the black revolution and the Negro revolution. Are they both the same? And if they're not, what is the difference? What is the difference between a black revolution and a Negro revolution? First, what is a revolution? Sometimes I'm inclined to believe that many of our people are using this word "revolution" loosely, without taking careful consideration of what this word actually means, and what its historic characteristics are. When you study the historic nature of revolutions, the motive of a revolution, the objective of a revolution, the result of a revolution, and the methods used in a revolution, you may change words. You may devise another program, you may change your goal and you may change your mind.

Look at the American Revolution in 1776. That revolution was for what? For land. Why did they want land? Independence. How was it carried out? Bloodshed. Number one, it was based on land, the basis of independence. And the only way they could get it was bloodshed. The French Revolution—what was it based on? The landless against the landlord. What was it for? Land. How did they get it? Bloodshed. Was no love lost, was no compromise, was no negotiation. I'm telling you—you don't know what a revolution is. Because when you find out what it is, you'll get back in the alley, you'll get out of the way.

The Russian Revolution—what was it based on? Land; the landless against the landlord. How did they bring it about? Bloodshed. You haven't got a revolution that doesn't involve bloodshed. And you're afraid to bleed. I said, you're afraid to bleed.

As long as the white man sent you to Korea, you bled. He sent you to Germany, you bled. He sent you to the South Pacific to fight the Japanese, you bled. You bleed for white people, but when it comes to seeing your own churches being bombed and little black girls murdered, you haven't got any blood. You bleed when the white man says bleed; you bite when the white man says bite; and you bark when the white man says bark. I hate to say this about us, but it's true. How are you going to be nonviolent in Mississippi, as violent as you were in Korea? How can you justify being nonviolent in Mississippi and Alabama, when your churches are being bombed, and your little girls are being murdered, and at the same time you are going to get violent with Hitler, and Tojo, and somebody else you don't even know?

If violence is wrong in America, violence is wrong abroad. If it is wrong to be violent defending black women and black children and black babies and black men, then it is wrong for America to draft us and make us violent abroad in defense of her. And if it is right for America to draft us, and teach us how to be violent in defense of her, then it is right for you and me to do whatever is necessary to defend our own people right here in this country. . . .

Of all our studies, history is best qualified to reward our research. And when you see that you've got problems, all you have to do is examine the historic method used all over the world by others who have problems similar to yours. Once you see how they got theirs straight, then you know how you can get yours straight. There's been a revolution, a black revolution, going on in Africa. In Kenya, the Mau Mau were revolutionary; they were the ones who brought the word "Uhuru" to the fore. The Mau Mau, they were revolutionary, they believed in scorched earth, they knocked everything aside that got in their way, and their revolution also was based on land, a desire for land. In Algeria, the northern part of Africa, a revolution took place. The Algerians were revolutionists, they wanted land. France offered to let them be integrated into France. They told France, to hell with France, they wanted some land, not some France. And they engaged in a bloody battle.

Nonviolence Is No Revolution

So I cite these various revolutions, brothers and sisters, to show you that you don't have a peaceful revolution. You don't have a turn-the-other-cheek revolution. There's no such thing as a nonviolent revolution. The only kind of revolution that is nonviolent is the Negro revolution. The only revolution in which the goal is loving your enemy is the Negro revolution. It's the only revolution in which the goal is a desegregated lunch counter, a desegregated theater, a desegregated park, and a desegregated public toilet; you can sit down next to white folks—on the toilet. That's no revolution. Revolution is based on land. Land is the basis of all independence. Land is the basis of freedom, justice, and equality.

The white man knows what a revolution is. He knows that the black revolution is world-wide in scope and in nature. The black revolution is sweeping Asia, is sweeping Africa, is rearing its head in Latin America. The Cuban Revolution—that's a revolution. They overturned the system. Revolution is in Asia, revolution is in Africa, and the white man is screaming because he sees revolution in Latin America. How do you think he'll react to you when you learn what a real revolution is? You don't know what a revolution is. If you did, you wouldn't use that word.

Revolution is bloody, revolution is hostile, revolution knows no compromise, revolution overturns and destroys everything that gets in its way. And you, sitting around here like a knot on the wall, saying, "I'm going to love these folks no matter how much they hate me." No, you need a revolution. Whoever heard of a revolution where they lock arms, as Rev. [Albert B.] Cleage was pointing out beautifully, singing "We Shall Overcome"? You don't do that in a revolution. You don't do any singing, you're too busy swinging. It's based on land. A revolutionary wants land so he can set up his own nation, an independent nation. These Negroes aren't asking for any nation—they're trying to crawl back on the plantation.

When you want a nation, that's called nationalism. When the white man became involved in a revolution in this country against England, what was it for? He wanted this land so he could set up another white nation. That's white nationalism. The American Revolution was white nationalism. The French Revolution was white nationalism. The Russian Revolution too—yes, it was—white nationalism. You don't think so? Why do you think Khrushchev and Mao can't get their heads together? White nationalism. All the revolutions that are going on in Asia and Africa today are based on what?—black nationalism. A revolutionary is a black nationalist. He wants a nation. I was reading some beautiful words by Rev. Cleage, pointing out why he couldn't get together with someone else in the city because all of them were afraid of being identified with black nationalism. If you're afraid of black nationalism, you're afraid of revolution. And if you love revolution, you love black nationalism.

The House Slave and the Field Slave

To understand this, you have to go back to what the young brother here referred to as the house Negro and the field Ne-

61

gro back during slavery. There were two kinds of slaves, the house Negro and the field Negro. The house Negroes—they lived in the house with master, they dressed pretty good, they ate good because they ate his food—what he left. They lived in the attic or the basement, but still they lived near the master; and they loved the master more than the master loved himself. They would give their life to save the master's house— quicker than the master would. If the master said, "We got a good house here," the house Negro would say, "Yeah, we got a good house here." Whenever the master said "we," he said "we." That's how you can tell a house Negro.

If the master's house caught on fire, the house Negro would fight harder to put the blaze out than the master would. If the master got sick, the house Negro would say, "What's the matter, boss, *we* sick?" *We* sick! He identified himself with his master, more than his master identified with himself. And if you came to the house Negro and said, "Let's run away, let's escape, let's separate," the house Negro would look at you and say, "Man, you crazy. What you mean, separate? Where is there a better house than this? Where can I wear better clothes than this? Where can I eat better food than this?" That was that house Negro. In those days he was called a "house nigger." And that's what we call them today, because we've still got some house niggers running around here.

This modern house Negro loves his master. He wants to live near him. He'll pay three times as much as the house is worth just to live near his master, and then brag about "I'm the only Negro out here." "I'm the only one on my job." "I'm the only one in this school." You're nothing but a house Negro. And if someone comes to you right now and says, "Let's separate," you say the same thing that the house Negro said on the plantation. "What you mean, separate? From America, this good white man? Where you going to get a better job than you get here?" I mean, this is what you say. "I ain't left nothing in Africa," that's what you say. Why, you left your mind in Africa.

On that same plantation, there was the field Negro. The field Negroes—those were the masses. There were always more Negroes in the field than there were Negroes in the house. The Negro in the field caught hell. He ate leftovers. In the house they ate high up on the hog. The Negro in the field didn't get anything but what was left of the insides of the hog. They call it "chitt'lings" nowadays. In those days they called them what they were—guts. That's what you were—gut-eaters. And some of you are still gut-eaters.

The field Negro was beaten from morning to night; he lived in a shack, in a hut; he wore old, castoff clothes. He hated his master. I say he hated his master. He was intelligent. That house Negro loved his master, but that field Negro— remember, they were in the majority, and they hated the master. When the house caught on fire, he didn't try to put it out; that field Negro prayed for a wind, for a breeze. When the master got sick, the field Negro prayed that he'd die. If someone came to the field Negro and said, "Let's separate, let's run," he didn't say "Where we going?" He'd say, "Any place is better than here." You've got field Negroes in America today. I'm a field Negro. The masses are the field Negroes. When they see this man's house on fire, you don't hear the little Negroes talking about "*our* government is in trouble." They say, "*The* government is in trouble." Imagine a Negro: "*Our* government"! I even heard one say "*our* astronauts." They won't even let him near the plant—and "*our* astronauts"! "*Our* Navy" —that's a Negro that is out of his mind, a Negro that is out of his mind.

Just as the slavemaster of that day used Tom, the house Negro, to keep the field Negroes in check, the same old slavemaster today has Negroes who are nothing but modern Uncle Toms, twentieth-century Uncle Toms, to keep you and me in check, to keep us under control, keep us passive and peaceful and nonviolent. That's Tom making you nonviolent. It's like when you go to the dentist, and the man's going to take your tooth. You're going to fight him when he starts pulling. So he squirts some stuff in your jaw called novocaine, to make you think they're not doing anything to you. So you sit there and because you've got all of that novocaine in your jaw, you suffer—peacefully. Blood running all down your jaw, and you don't know what's happening. Because someone has taught you to suffer—peacefully.

The white man does the same thing to you in the street, when he wants to put knots on your head and take advantage of you and not have to be afraid of your fighting back. To keep you from fighting back, he gets these old religious Uncle Toms to teach you and me, just like novocaine, to suffer peacefully. Don't stop suffering—just suffer peacefully. As Rev. Cleage pointed out, they say you should let your blood flow in the streets. This is a shame. You know he's a Christian preacher. If it's a shame to him, you know what it is to me.

There is nothing in our book, the Koran, that teaches us to suffer peacefully. Our religion teaches us to be intelligent. Be peaceful, be courteous, obey the law, respect everyone; but if someone puts his hand on you, send him to the cemetery. That's a good religion. In fact, that's that old-time religion. That's the one that Ma and Pa used to talk about: an eye for an eye, and a tooth for a tooth, and a head for a head, and a life for a life. That's a good religion. And nobody resents that kind of religion being taught but a wolf, who intends to make you his meal.

This is the way it is with the white man in America. He's a wolf—and you're sheep. Any time a shepherd, a pastor, teaches you and me not to run from the white man and, at the same time, teaches us not to fight the white man, he's a traitor to you and me. Don't lay down a life all by itself. No, preserve your life, it's the best thing you've got. And if you've got to give it up, let it be even-steven.

Blacks Must Develop Their Community

Stokely Carmichael

By the mid-1960s some young American blacks were losing patience with the slow progress of the civil rights movement. Instead, they looked to younger, more militaristic leaders like Stokely Carmichael. Born in Trinidad in 1941, he joined the Student Nonviolent Coordinating Committee (SNCC) in 1964, becoming its president in 1966. He coined the phrase "Black Power," which encapsulated the idea that blacks should take control of every aspect of their lives by any means necessary (including violence) and should abandon efforts to integrate with white society.

Carmichael's philosophy is spelled out in the following essay, written by Carmichael in 1966. He suggests that the Black Power Movement has been misrepresented in the media, that integration is not possible, and that black communities must unite to achieve equality.

In 1969 Carmichael moved with his wife to Guinea, West Africa, where he became an aide to the nation's prime minister. In 1978 he changed his name to Kwame Ture to honor two African leaders. He died in Guinea in 1998.

In this "debate," as in everything else that affects our lives, Negroes are dependent on, and at the discretion of, forces and institutions within the white society which have little interest in representing us honestly. Our experience with the national press has been that where they have managed to escape a meretricious special interest in "Git Whitey" sensationalism and race-war mongering, individual reporters and commentators have been conditioned by the enveloping racism of the

Stokely Carmichael, "Toward Black Liberation," *Massachusetts Review*, vol. 7, Autumn 1966, pp. 643–51. Reproduced by permission of Michael Thelwell.

society to the point where they are incapable even of objective observation and reporting of racial *incidents*, much less the analysis of *ideas*. But this limitation of vision and perceptions is an inevitable consequence of the dictatorship of definition, interpretation, and consciousness, along with the censorship of history that the society has inflicted upon the Negro—and itself. . . .

Defining the Struggle

We shall have to struggle for the right to create our own terms through which to define ourselves and our relationship to the society, and to have these terms recognized. This is the first necessity of a free people, and the first right that any oppressor must suspend. The white fathers of American racism knew this—instinctively it seems—as is indicated by the continuous record of the distortion and omission in their dealings with the red and black men. In the same way that southern apologists for the "Jim Crow" society have so obscured, muddied and misrepresented the record of the reconstruction period, until it is almost impossible to tell what really happened, their contemporary counterparts are busy doing the same thing with the recent history of the civil rights movement.

In 1964, for example, the National Democratic Party, led by L. B. Johnson and Hubert H. Humphrey, cynically undermined the efforts of Mississippi's Black population to achieve some degree of political representation. Yet, whenever the events of that convention are recalled by the press, one sees only that version fabricated by the press agents of the Democratic Party. A year later the House of Representatives in an even more vulgar display of political racism made a mockery of the political rights of Mississippi's Negroes when it failed to unseat the Mississippi Delegation to the House which had been elected through a process which methodically and systematically excluded over 450,000 voting age Negroes, almost one half of the total electorate of the state. Whenever this event is mentioned in print it is in terms which leaves one with the rather curious impression that somehow the oppressed Negro people of Mississippi are at fault for confronting the Congress with a situation in which they had no alternative but to endorse Mississippi's racist political practices.

I mention these two examples because, having been directly involved in them, I can see very clearly the discrepancies between what happened, and the versions that are finding their way into general acceptance as a kind of popular mythology. Thus the victimization of the Negro takes place in two phases—first it occurs in fact and deed, then, and this is equally sinister, in the official recording of those facts.

Misrepresentation of Black Power

The "Black Power" program and concept which is being articulated by SNCC [Student Nonviolent Coordinating Committee], CORE [Congress of Racial Equality], and a host of community organizations in the ghettoes of the North and South has not escaped that process. The white press has been busy articulating their own analyses, their own interpretations, and criticisms of their own creations. For example, while the press had given wide and sensational dissemination to attacks made by figures in the Civil Rights movement—foremost among which are Roy Wilkins of the NAACP [National Association for the Advancement of Colored People] and Whitney Young of the Urban League—and to the hysterical ranting about black racism made by the political chameleon that now serves as Vice-President [Hubert H. Humphrey], it has generally failed to give accounts of the reasonable and productive dialogue which is taking place in the Negro community, and in certain important areas in the white religious and intellectual community. A national committee of influential Negro Churchmen affiliated with the National Council of Churches, despite their oblivious respectability and responsibility, had to resort to a paid advertisement to articulate their position, while anyone shouting the hysterical yappings of "Black Racism" got ample space. Thus the American people have gotten at best a superficial and misleading account of the very terms and tenor of this debate. I wish to quote briefly from the statement by the national committee of Churchmen which I suspect that the majority of Americans will not have seen. This statement appeared in the *New York Times* of July 31, 1966.

> *We an informal group of Negro Churchmen in America are deeply disturbed about the crisis brought upon our country by historic distortions of important human realities in the controversy about "black power." What we see shining through the variety of rhetoric is not anything new but the same old problem of power and race which has faced our beloved country since 1619.*
>
> *. . . The conscience of black men is corrupted because, having no power to implement the demands of conscience, the concern for justice in the absence of justice becomes a chaotic self-surrender. Powerlessness breeds a race of beggars. We are faced now with a situation where powerless conscience meets conscienceless power, threatening the very foundations of our Nation.*
>
> . . . We deplore the overt violence of riots, but we feel it is more important to focus on the real sources of these eruptions. These sources may be abetted inside the Ghetto, but their basic cause lies in the silent and covert violence which white middleclass America inflicts upon the victims of the inner city. . . .

Institutionalized Racism

The history of every institution of this society indicates that a major concern in the ordering and structuring of the society has been the maintaining of the Negro community in its condition of dependence and oppression. This has not been on the level of individual acts of discrimination between individual whites against individual Negroes, but as total acts by the White community against the Negro community. This fact cannot be too strongly emphasized—the racist assumptions of white superiority have been so deeply ingrained in the structure of the society that it infuses its entire functioning, and is so much a part of the national subconscious that it is taken for granted and is frequently not even recognized.

Let me give an example of the difference between individual racism and institutionalized racism, and the society's response to both. When unidentified white terrorists bomb a Negro Church and kill five children, that is an act of individual racism, widely deplored by most segments of the society. But when in that same city, Birmingham, Alabama, not five but 500 Negro babies die each year because of a lack of proper food, shelter and medical facilities, and thousands more are destroyed and maimed physically, emotionally and intellectually because of conditions of poverty and deprivation in the ghetto, that is a function of institutionalized racism. But the society either pretends it doesn't know of this situation, or is incapable of doing anything meaningful about it. And this resistance to doing anything meaningful about conditions in that ghetto comes from the fact that the ghetto is itself a product of a combination of forces and special interests in the white community, and the groups that have access to the resources and power to change that situation benefit, politically and economically, from the existence of that ghetto.

It is more than a figure of speech to say that the Negro community in America is the victim of white imperialism and colonial exploitation. This is in practical economic and political terms true. There are over 20 million black people comprising ten percent of this nation. They for the most part live in well-defined areas of the country—in the shanty-towns and rural black belt areas of the South, and increasingly in the slums of northern and western industrial cities. If one goes into any Negro community, whether it be in Jackson, Miss.,

Cambridge, Md., or Harlem, N.Y., one will find that the same combination of political, economic, and social forces are at work. The people in the Negro community do not control the resources of that community, its political decisions, its law enforcement, its housing standards; and even the physical ownership of the land, houses, and stores *lie outside that community.*

It is white power that makes the laws, and it is violent white power in the form of armed white cops that enforces those laws with guns and nightsticks. The vast majority of Negroes in this country live in these captive communities and must endure these conditions of oppression because, and only because, *they are black and powerless.* I do not suppose that at any point the men who control the power and resources of this country ever sat down and designed these black enclaves, and formally articulated the terms of their colonial and dependent status, as was done, for example, by the Apartheid government of South Africa. Yet, one can not distinguish between one ghetto and another. As one moves from city to city it is as though some malignant racist planning-unit had done precisely this—designed each one from the same master blueprint. And indeed, if the ghetto had been formally and deliberately planned, instead of growing spontaneously and inevitably from the racist functioning of the various institutions that combine to make the society, it would be somehow less frightening. The situation would be less frightening because, if these ghettoes were the result of design and conspiracy, one could understand their similarity as being artificial and consciously imposed, rather than the result of identical patterns of white racism which repeat themselves in cities as distant as Boston and Birmingham. . . .

The Failure to Integrate Communities

In recent years the answer to these questions which has been given by most articulate groups of Negroes and their white allies, the "liberals" of all stripes, has been in terms of something called "integration." According to the advocates of integration, social justice will be accomplished by "integrating the Negro into the mainstream institutions of the society from which he has been traditionally excluded." It is very significant that each time I have heard this formulation it has been in terms of "the Negro," the individual Negro, rather than in terms of the community.

The concept of integration had to be based on the assumption that there was nothing of value in the Negro community and that little of value could be created among Negroes, so the thing to do was to siphon off the "acceptable" Negroes into the surrounding middle-class white community. Thus the goal of the movement for integration was simply to loosen up the restrictions barring the entry of Negroes into the white community. Goals around which the struggle took place, such as public accommodation, open housing, job opportunity on the executive level (which is easier to deal with than the problem of semiskilled and blue collar jobs which involve more far-reaching economic adjustments), are quite simply middle-class goals, articulated by a tiny group of Negroes who had middle-class aspirations. It is true that the student demonstrations in the South during the early sixties, out of which SNCC came, had a similar orientation. But while it is hardly a concern of a black sharecropper, dishwasher, or welfare recipient whether a certain fifteen-dollar-a-day motel offers accommodations to Negroes, the overt symbols of white superiority and the imposed limitations on the Negro community had to be destroyed. Now, black people must look beyond these goals, to the issue of collective power.

Such a limited class orientation was reflected not only in the program and goals of the civil rights movement, but in its tactics and organization. It is very significant that the two oldest and most "respectable" civil rights organizations have constitutions which *specifically* prohibit partisan political activity.

CORE once did, but changed that clause when it changed its orientation toward black power. But this is perfectly understandable in terms of the strategy and goals of the older organizations. The civil rights movement saw its role as a kind of liaison between the powerful white community and the dependent Negro one. The dependent status of the black community apparently was unimportant since—if the movement were successful—it was going to blend into the white community anyway. We made no pretense of organizing and developing institutions of community power in the Negro community, but appealed to the conscience of white institutions of power. The posture of the civil rights movement was that of the dependent, the suppliant. The theory was that without attempting to create any organized base of political strength itself, the civil rights movement could, by forming coalitions with various "liberal" pressure organizations in the white community—liberal reform clubs, labor unions, church groups, progressive civic groups—and at times one or other of the major political parties—influence national legislation and national social patterns.

The Limitations of Good-will

I think we all have seen the limitations of this approach. We have repeatedly seen that political alliances based on appeals to conscience and decency are chancy things, simply because institutions and political organizations have no consciences outside their own special interests. The political and social rights of Negroes have been and always will be negotiable and expendable the moment they conflict with the interests of our "allies." If we do not learn from history, we are doomed to repeat it, and that is precisely the lesson of the Reconstruction. Black people were allowed to register, vote and participate in politics because it was to the advantage of powerful white allies to promote this. But this was the result of white decision, and it was ended by other white men's decision before any political base powerful enough to challenge that decision could be established in the southern Negro community. (Thus at this point in the struggle Negroes have no assurance—save a kind of idiot optimism and faith in a society whose history is one of racism—that if it were to become necessary, even the painfully limited gains thrown to the civil rights movement by the Congress will not be revoked as soon as a shift in political sentiments should occur.)

The major limitation of this approach was that it tended to maintain the traditional dependence of Negroes, and of the movement. We depended upon the good-will and support of various groups within the white community whose interests were not always compatible with ours. To the extent that we depended on the financial support of other groups, we were vulnerable to their influence and domination.

Results of Integration

The fact is that what must be abolished is not the black community, but the dependent colonial status that has been inflicted upon it. The racial and cultural personality of the black community must be preserved and the community must win its freedom while preserving its cultural integrity. This is the essential difference between integration as it is currently practiced and the concept of black power.

What has the movement for integration accomplished to date? The Negro graduating from M.I.T. with a doctorate will have better job opportunities available to him than to Lynda Bird Johnson. But the rate of unemployment in the Negro community is steadily increasing, while that in the white community decreases. More educated Negroes hold executive jobs in major corporations and federal agencies than ever before, but the gap between white income and Negro income has almost doubled in the last twenty years. More suburban housing is available to Negroes, but housing conditions in the ghetto are steadily declining. While the infant mortality rate of

New York City is at its lowest rate ever in the city's history, the infant mortality rate of Harlem is steadily climbing. There has been an organized national resistance to the Supreme Court's order to integrate the schools, and the federal government has not acted to enforce that order. Less than 15 percent of black children in the South attend integrated schools; and Negro schools, which the vast majority of black children still attend, are increasingly decrepit, overcrowded, under-staffed, inadequately equipped and funded.

This explains why the rate of school dropouts is increasing among Negro teenagers, who then express their bitterness, hopelessness, and alienation by the only means they have—rebellion. As long as people in the ghettoes of our large cities feel that they are victims of the misuse of white power without any way to have their needs represented—and these are frequently simple needs: to get the welfare inspectors to stop kicking down your doors in the middle of the night, the cops from beating your children, the landlord to exterminate the vermin in your home, the city to collect your garbage—we will continue to have riots. These are not the products of "black power," but of the absence of any organization capable of giving the community the power, the black power, to deal with its problems.

Communities Must Organize

SNCC proposes that it is now time for the black freedom movement to stop pandering to the fears and anxieties of the white middle class in the attempt to earn its "good-will," and to return to the ghetto to organize these communities to control themselves. This organization must be attempted in northern and southern urban areas as well as in the rural black belt counties of the South. The chief antagonist to this organization is, in the South, the overtly racist Democratic party, and in the North the equally corrupt big city machines.

The standard argument presented against independent political organization is "But you are only 10 percent." I cannot see the relevance of this observation, since no one is talking about taking over the country, but taking control over our own communities.

The fact is that the Negro population, 10 percent or not, is very strategically placed because—ironically—of segregation. What is also true is that Negroes have never been able to utilize the full voting potential of our numbers. Where we could vote, the case has always been that the white political machine stacks and gerrymanders the political subdivisions in Negro neighborhoods so the true voting strength is never reflected in political strength. Would anyone looking at the distribution of political power in Manhattan, ever think that Negroes represented 60 percent of the population there?

Just as often the effective political organization in Negro communities is absorbed by tokenism and patronage—the time honored practice of "giving" certain offices to selected Negroes. The machine thus creates a "little machine," which is subordinate and responsive to it, in the Negro community. These Negro political "leaders" are really vote deliverers, more responsible to the white machine and the white power structure, than to the community they allegedly represent. Thus the white community is able to substitute patronage control for audacious black power in the Negro community. . . .

Success Depends on Leadership and Organization

We must organize black community power to end these abuses, and to give the Negro community a chance to have its needs expressed. A leadership which is truly "responsible" —not to the white press and power structure, but to the community—must be developed. Such leadership will recognize that its power lies in the unified and collective strength of that community. This will make it difficult for the white leadership group to conduct its dialogue with individuals in terms of patronage and prestige, and will force them to talk to the community's representatives in terms of real power.

The single aspect of the black power program that has encountered most criticism is this concept of independent organization. This is presented as third-partyism which has never worked, or a withdrawal into black nationalism and isolationism. If such a program is developed it will not have the effect of isolating the Negro community but the reverse. When the Negro community is able to control local office, and negotiate with other groups from a position of organized strength, the possibility of meaningful political alliances on specific issues will be increased. That is a rule of politics and there is no reason why it should not operate here. The only difference is that we will have the power to define the terms of these alliances.

The next question usually is, "So—can it work, can the ghettoes in fact be organized?" The answer is that this organization must be successful, because there are no viable alternatives—not the War on Poverty, which was at its inception limited to dealing with effects rather than causes, and has become simply another source of machine patronage. And "Integration" is meaningful only to a small chosen class within the community.

The revolution in agricultural technology in the South is displacing the rural Negro community into northern urban areas. Both Washington, D.C. and Newark, N.J. have Negro majorities. One third of Philadelphia's population of two million people is black. "Inner city" in most major urban areas is already predominantly Negro, and with the white rush to suburbia, Negroes will in the next three decades control the heart of our great cities. These areas can become either concentration camps with a bitter and volatile population whose only power is the power to destroy, or organized and powerful communities able to make constructive contributions to the total society. Without the power to control their lives and their communities, without effective political institutions through which to relate to the total society, these communities will exist in a constant state of insurrection. This is a choice that the country will have to make.

Blacks Will Lead the Way to Rights Beyond Civil Liberties

A. Philip Randolph

In 1941, A. Philip Randolph planned a march on Washington to end employment discrimination. Before the march was held, however, President Franklin D. Roosevelt signed an order to end discrimination in defense plant jobs, and the march was cancelled. Just 22 years later, Randolph was again at the forefront of a march on Washington—this time the organizers would not be deterred by the promises of politicians. On August 28, 1963, Randolph made the following speech before a crowd of more than 250,000.

Fellow Americans, we are gathered here in the largest demonstration in the history of this nation. Let the nation and world know the meaning of our numbers. We are not a pressure group. We are not an organization or a group of organizations. We are not a mob. We are the advance guard of a massive moral revolution for jobs and freedom.

This revolution reverberates throughout the land, touching every city, every town, every village where black men are segregated, oppressed, and exploited. But this civil rights revolution is not confined to the Negro nor is it confined to civil rights, for our white allies know that they cannot be free while we are not; and we know we have no future in a society in which six million black and white people are unemployed and millions more live in poverty. Nor is the goal of our civil rights revolution merely the passage of civil rights legislation.

Beyond Civil Rights Legislation

Yes, we want all public accommodations open to all citizens, but those accommodations will mean little to those who cannot afford to use them. Yes, we want a Fair Employment Prac-

A. Philip Randolph, "Address at the 1963 March on Washington," August 28, 1963.

tices Act, but what good will it do to millions of workers, black and white? We want integrated public schools, but that means we also wanted federal aid to education—all forms of education. We want a free democratic society dedicated to the political, economic, and social advancement of man along moral lines. Now, we know that real freedom will require many changes in the nation's political and social philosophies and institutions. For one thing, we must destroy the notion that Mrs. Murphy's property rights include the right to humiliate me because of the color of my skin. The sanctity of private property takes second place to the sanctity of the human personality.

It falls to the Negro to reassert this proper priority of values because our ancestors were transformed from human personalities into private poetry. It falls to us to demand new forms of social planning, to create full employment, and to put automation at the service of human needs, not at the service of profits—for we are the first victims of unemployment. Negroes are in the forefront of today's movement for social and racial justice because we know we cannot expect the realization of our aspirations through the same old anti-democratic social institutions and philosophies that have all along frustrated our aspirations.

And so we have taken our struggle into the streets, as the labor movement took its struggle into the streets, as Jesus Christ led the multitudes through the streets of Judea. The plain and simple fact is that until we went into the streets the federal government was indifferent to our demands. It was not until the streets and jails of Birmingham were filled that Congress began to think about civil rights legislation. It was not until thousands demonstrated in the South that lunch counters and other public accommodations were integrated. It was not until the freedom riders were brutalized in Alabama that the 1964 Supreme Court decision banning discrimination in interstate travel was enforced, and it was not until construction sites were picketed in the North that Negro workers were hired.

No Peace Without Justice

Those who deplore our militancy, who exhort patience in the name of a false peace, are in fact supporting segregation and exploitation. They would have social peace at the expense of social and racial justice. They are more concerned with easing racial tensions than with enforcing racial democracy. The months and years ahead will bring new evidence of masses in motion for freedom. The March on Washington is not the climax of our struggle but a new beginning, not only for the Negro but for all Americans who thirst for freedom and a better life.

Look for the enemies of Medicare, for high minimum wages, of social security, of federal aid to education, and there you will find the enemy of the Negro—the coalition of Dixiecrats and reactionary Republicans that seek to dominate the Congress. We must develop strength in order that we may be able to back and support the civil rights program of President Kennedy. In the struggle against these forces, all of us should be prepared to take to the streets. The spirit and techniques that built the labor movement, founded churches, and now guide the civil rights evolution must be a massive crusade, must be launched against the unholy coalition of Dixiecrats and the racists that seek to strangle Congress.

We here today are only the first wave. When we leave, it will be to carry the civil rights revolution home with us into every nook and cranny of the land, and we shall return again and again to Washington in very growing numbers until total freedom is ours. We shall settle for nothing less, and may God grant that we may have the courage, the strength, and the faith in this hour of trial by fire never to falter.

CHAPTER 3

Foot Soldiers in the Movement: Voices from the Front Lines

Confronting Racism at Little Rock's Central High School

Daisy Bates

When the Supreme Court ordered the end of segregated schools in 1954, it set the stage for conflict in the South. The first major confrontation came in 1957 in Little Rock, Arkansas. On September 4, facing angry mobs of white supremacists, nine black students tried to enter Central High School but were turned away. Not until September 25, and then only with a military escort sent by President Dwight D. Eisenhower, did all nine succeed in attending classes. Daisy Bates, Little Rock resident, president of the state's NAACP chapter, and editor in chief of the black newspaper Arkansas State Press, *wrote of her experiences during this frightening time.*

In her memoirs she wrote about trying to see that those selected to integrate Central High—Carlotta Walls, Jefferson Thomas, Elizabeth Eckford, Thelma Mothershed, Melba Pattillo, Ernest Green, Terrance Roberts, Gloria Ray, and Minnijean Brown—made it safely to school. Following is her account of that first day of school, September 4, focusing primarily on the experiences of Elizabeth Eckford, who was separated from the others and had to run her gauntlet alone. Television cameras, reporters, and photographers from around the world recorded the event. For many across the country it was their first look at the rabid racial prejudice southern blacks had to live with.

I don't recall all the details of what Governor [Orval] Faubus said that night [September 2, 1957]. But his words electrified Little Rock. By morning they shocked the United States. By noon the next day his message horrified the world.

Faubus' alleged reason for calling out the troops [National Guard] was that he had received information that caravans of automobiles filled with white supremacists were heading toward Little Rock from all over the state. He therefore declared Central High School off limits to Negroes. For some inexplicable reason he added that Horace Mann, a Negro high school, would be off limits to whites.

Then, from the chair of the highest office of the State of Arkansas, Governor Orval Eugene Faubus delivered the infamous words, "blood will run in the streets" if Negro pupils should attempt to enter Central High School.

In a half dozen ill-chosen words, Faubus made his contribution to the mass hysteria that was to grip the city of Little Rock for several months. . . .

Calls for Help

I called the city police. I explained to the officer in charge that we were concerned about the safety of the children and that we were trying to get ministers to accompany them to school the next morning [September 4]. I said that the children would assemble at eight-thirty at Twelfth Street and Park Avenue. I asked whether a police car could be stationed there to protect the children until the ministers arrived.

The police officer promised to have a squad car there at eight o'clock. "But you realize," he warned, "that our men cannot go any closer than that to the school. The school is off limits to the city police while it's 'occupied' by the Arkansas National Guardsmen."

By now it was two-thirty in the morning. Still, the parents had to be called about the change in plan. At three o'clock I completed my last call, explaining to the parents where the children were to assemble and the plan about the ministers. Suddenly I remembered Elizabeth Eckford. Her family had no telephone. Should I go to the Union Station and search for her father? Someone had once told me that he had a night job there. Tired in mind and body, I decided to handle the matter early in the morning. I stumbled into bed.

A few hours later, at about eight fifteen in the morning, [my husband] L.C. and I started driving to Twelfth Street and Park Avenue. On the way I checked out in my mind the possibilities that awaited us. The ministers might be there—or again they might not. Mr. Ogden [Rev. Dunbar Ogden Jr., president of the Little Rock Interracial Ministerial Alliance] failing to find anyone to accompany him, understandably might not arrive. Would the police be there? How many? And what if—?

The bulletin over the car radio interrupted. The voice announced: "A Negro girl is being mobbed at Central High. . . ."

"Oh, my God!" I cried. "It must be Elizabeth! I forgot to notify her where to meet us!"

L.C. jumped out of the car and rushed to find her. I drove on to Twelfth Street. There were the ministers—two white— Mr. Ogden and Rev. Will Campbell, of the National Council of Churches, Nashville, Tennessee—and two colored—the Reverend Z. Z. Driver, of the African Methodist Episcopal Church, and the Reverend Harry Bass, of the Methodist Church. With them also was Mr. Ogden's twenty-one-year-old son, David. The children were already there. And, yes, the police had come as promised. All of the children were there—all except Elizabeth.

Soon L.C. rushed up with the news that Elizabeth finally was free of the mob. He had seen her on a bus as it pulled away.

Trying to Enter the School

The children set out, two ministers in front of them, two behind. They proceeded in that formation until they approached the beginning of the long line of guardsmen. At this point they had their first brush with the mob. They were jostled and shoved. As they made their way toward the school grounds, the ministers and their charges attempted to pass the guardsmen surrounding Central High. A National Guard captain stopped them. He told Mr. Ogden he could not allow them to pass through the guard line. When Mr. Ogden asked why, the captain said it was by order of Governor Faubus.

The ministers returned to the car with the students and Mr. Ogden reported what the captain of the guardsmen had said. . . .

A Reporter's Experience

Dr. Benjamin Fine was then education editor of *The New York Times*. He had years before won for his newspaper a Pulitzer prize. He was among the first reporters on the scene to cover the Little Rock story.

A few days after the National Guard blocked the Negro children's entrance to the school, Ben showed up at my house. He paced the floor nervously, rubbing his hands together as he talked.

"Daisy, they spat in my face. They called me a 'dirty Jew.' I've been a marked man ever since the day Elizabeth tried to enter Central. I never told you what happened that day. I tried not to think about it. Maybe I was ashamed to admit to you or to myself that white men and women could be so beastly cruel.

"I was standing in front of the school that day. Suddenly there was a shout—'They're here! The niggers are coming!' I saw a sweet little girl who looked about fifteen, walking alone. She tried several times to pass through the guards. The last time she tried, they put their bayonets in front of her. When they did this, she became panicky. For a moment she just stood there trembling. Then she seemed to calm down and started walking toward the bus stop with the mob baying at her heels like a pack of hounds. The women were shouting, 'Get her! Lynch her!' The men were yelling, 'Go home, you bastard of a black bitch!' She finally made it to the bus stop and sat down on the bench. I sat down beside her and said, 'I'm a reporter from *The New York Times*, may I have your name?' She just sat there, her head down. Tears were streaming down her cheeks from under her sun glasses. Daisy, I don't know what made me put my arm around her, lifting her chin, saying, 'Don't let them see you cry.' Maybe she reminded me of my fifteen-year-old daughter, Jill.

Trying to Help

"There must have been five hundred around us by this time. I vaguely remember someone hollering, 'Get a rope and drag her over to this tree.' Suddenly I saw a white-haired, kind-faced woman fighting her way through the mob. She looked at Elizabeth, and then screamed at the mob, 'Leave this child alone! Why are you tormenting her? Six months from now, you will hang your heads in shame.' The mob shouted, 'Another nigger-lover. Get out of here!' The woman, who I found out later was Mrs. Grace Lorch, the wife of Dr. Lee Lorch, professor at Philander Smith College, turned to me and said, 'We have to do something. Let's try to get a cab.'

"We took Elizabeth across the street to the drugstore. I remained on the sidewalk with Elizabeth while Mrs. Lorch tried to enter the drugstore to call a cab. But the hoodlums slammed the door in her face and wouldn't let her in. She pleaded with them to call a cab for the child. They closed in on her saying, 'Get out of here, you bitch! Just then the city bus came. Mrs. Lorch and Elizabeth got on. Elizabeth must have been in a state of shock. She never uttered a word. When the bus pulled away, the mob closed in around me. 'We saw you put your arm around that little bitch. Now it's your turn.' A drab, middle-aged woman said viciously, 'Grab him and kick him in the balls!' A girl I had seen hustling in one of the local bars screamed, 'A dirty New York Jew! Get him!' A man asked me, 'Are you a Jew?' I said, 'Yes.' He then said to the mob, 'Let him be! We'll take care of him later.'

"The irony of it all, Daisy, is that during all this time the national guardsmen made no effort to protect Elizabeth or to help me. Instead, they threatened to have me arrested—for inciting to riot."

Struggling to Describe the Events

Elizabeth, whose dignity and control in the face of jeering mobsters had been filmed by television cameras and recorded in pictures flashed to newspapers over the world, had overnight become a national heroine. During the next few days newspaper reporters besieged her home, wanting to talk to her. The first day that her parents agreed she might come out of seclusion, she came to my house where the reporters awaited her. Elizabeth was very quiet, speaking only when spoken to. I took her to my bedroom to talk before I let the reporters see her. I asked how she felt now. Suddenly all her pent-up emotion flared.

"Why am I here?" she said, turning blazing eyes on me. "Why are you so interested in my welfare now? You didn't care enough to notify me of the change of plans—"

I walked over and reached out to her. Before she turned her back on me, I saw tears gathering in her eyes. My heart was breaking for this young girl who stood there trying to stifle her sobs. How could I explain that frantic early morning when at three o'clock my mind had gone on strike?

In the ensuing weeks Elizabeth took part in all the activities of the nine—press conferences, attendance at court, studying with professors at nearby Philander Smith College. She was present, that is, but never really a part of things. The hurt had been too deep.

On the two nights she stayed at my home I was awakened by the screams in her sleep, as she relived in her dreams the terrifying mob scenes at Central. The only times Elizabeth showed real excitement were when [NAACP attorney and future Supreme Court justice] Thurgood Marshall met the children and explained the meaning of what had happened in court. As he talked, she would listen raptly, a faint smile on her face. It was obvious he was her hero.

Little by little Elizabeth came out of her shell. Up to now she had never talked about what happened to her at Central. Once when we were alone in the downstairs recreation room of my house, I asked her simply, "Elizabeth, do you think you can talk about it now?"

She remained quiet for a long time. Then she began to speak.

"You remember the day before we were to go in, we met [Little Rock School] Superintendent [Virgil T.] Blossom at the school board office. He told us what the mob might say and do but he never told us we wouldn't have any protection. He told our parents not to come because he wouldn't be able to protect the children if they did.

"That night I was so excited I couldn't sleep. The next morning I was about the first one up. While I was pressing my black and white dress—I had made it to wear on the first day of school—my little brother turned on the TV set. They started telling about a large crowd gathered at the school. The man on TV said he wondered if we were going to show up that morning. Mother called from the kitchen, where she was fixing breakfast, 'Turn that TV off!' She was so upset and worried. I wanted to comfort her, so I said, 'Mother, don't worry.'

"Dad was walking back and forth, from room to room, with a sad expression. He was chewing on his pipe and he had a cigar in his hand, but he didn't light either one. It would have been funny, only he was so nervous.

Elizabeth's Ordeal

"Before I left home Mother called us into the living-room. She said we should have a word of prayer. Then I caught the bus and got off a block from the school. I saw a large crowd of people standing across the street from the soldiers guarding

Central. As I walked on, the crowd suddenly got very quiet. Superintendent Blossom had told us to enter by the front door. I looked at all the people and thought, 'Maybe I will be safer if I walk down the block to the front entrance behind the guards.'

"At the corner I tried to pass through the long line of guards around the school so as to enter the grounds behind them. One of the guards pointed across the street. So I pointed in the same direction and asked whether he meant for me to cross the street and walk down. He nodded 'yes.' So, I walked across the street conscious of the crowd that stood there, but they moved away from me.

"For a moment all I could hear was the shuffling of their feet. Then someone shouted, 'Here she comes, get ready!' I moved away from the crowd on the sidewalk and into the street. If the mob came at me I could then cross back over so the guards could protect me.

"The crowd moved in closer and then began to follow me, calling me names. I still wasn't afraid. Just a little bit nervous. Then my knees started to shake all of a sudden and I wondered whether I could make it to the center entrance a block away. It was the longest block I ever walked in my whole life.

Blocked by the Guards

"Even so, I still wasn't too scared because all the time I kept thinking that the guards would protect me.

"When I got right in front of the school, I went up to a guard again. But this time he just looked straight ahead and didn't move to let me pass him. I didn't know what to do. Then I looked and saw that the path leading to the front entrance was a little further ahead. So I walked until I was right in front of the path to the front door.

"I stood looking at the school—it looked so big! Just then the guards let some white students go through.

"The crowd was quiet. I guess they were waiting to see what was going to happen. When I was able to steady my knees, I walked up to the guard who had let the white students in. He too didn't move. When I tried to squeeze past him, he raised his bayonet and then the other guards closed in and they raised their bayonets.

"They glared at me with a mean look and I was very frightened and didn't know what to do. I turned around and the crowd came toward me.

"They moved closer and closer. Somebody started yelling, 'Lynch her! Lynch her!'

"I tried to see a friendly face somewhere in the mob—someone who maybe would help. I looked into the face of an old woman and it seemed a kind face, but when I looked at her again, she spat on me.

"They came closer, shouting, 'No nigger bitch is going to get in our school. Get out of here!'

"I turned back to the guards but their faces told me I wouldn't get help from them. Then I looked down the block and saw a bench at the bus stop. I thought, 'If I can only get there I will be safe.' I don't know why the bench seemed a safe place to me, but I started walking toward it. I tried to close my mind to what they were shouting, and kept saying to myself, 'If I can only make it to the bench I will be safe.'

"When I finally got there, I don't think I could have gone another step. I sat down and the mob crowded up and began shouting all over again. Someone hollered, 'Drag her over to this tree! Let's take care of the nigger.' Just then a white man sat down beside me, put his arm around me and patted my shoulder. He raised my chin and said, 'Don't let them see you cry.'

"Then, a white lady—she was very nice—she came over to me on the bench. She spoke to me but I don't remember now what she said. She put me on the bus and sat next to me. She asked me my name and tried to talk to me but I don't think I answered. I can't remember much about the bus ride, but the next thing I remember I was standing in front of the School for the Blind, where Mother works.

"I thought, 'Maybe she isn't here. But she has to be here!' So I ran upstairs, and I think some teachers tried to talk to me, but I kept running until I reached Mother's classroom.

"Mother was standing at the window with her head bowed, but she must have sensed I was there because she turned around. She looked as if she had been crying, and I wanted to tell her I was all right. But I couldn't speak. She put her arms around me and I cried."

Black Students Take a Stand: Sit-ins and Freedom Rides

Diane Nash

Diane Nash is one of the unsung heroes of the American civil rights movement. Born in Chicago, she had never suffered the indignities of full-blown racial segregation until she went to college in Nashville, Tennessee. In 1960, as an undergraduate at Fisk University, she participated in civil rights demonstrations with fellow students, successfully desegregating Nashville lunch counters. In the same year, she helped found the Student Nonviolent Coordinating Committee (SNCC), the student arm of the civil rights movement.

In 1961 she led a large contingent of Freedom Riders—students riding buses through the Deep South to protest segregated buses, restrooms, waiting rooms, and other public facilities. In the following selection she recalls her experiences as a student at Nashville sit-ins, as a SNCC organizer, and, later, at the age of twenty-three (and six months pregnant), as a "criminal" arrested in Jackson, Mississippi, and jailed for encouraging younger demonstrators to break local segregation laws.

I grew up on the South Side of Chicago, and while there was segregation there, I didn't really notice it that much. I always knew things were much worse in the South, because my father was a dining car waiter, and he would often come home and tell us about how hard it was to find a hotel down there that would accommodate Negroes, as we were called at that time. While I ran into some discrimination growing up, it wasn't until I went to school in Nashville, Tennessee, that I experienced real segregation. When I arrived at Fisk University, I spent the first month or so on campus. When I did venture out, I visited a few of the places near campus that were available to blacks, but everything else was segregated. After a few weeks, when the novelty was wearing off, I really started to feel limited. I resented not being able to go downtown to the Woolworth's and have lunch with a friend. Also, when I was downtown, I saw lots of blacks sitting out on the curb or on the ground eating their lunches because they weren't allowed to sit in the restaurants and eat. It was so demeaning. The first time I had to use a women's restroom marked "colored" was pretty humiliating, too. I was at the state fair with a young man, and when I came back from the restroom I was really fuming. This man was from Tennessee, and he said something like, "Are you really that upset?" And I said yes, I really was.

Taking Action

Pretty soon I started looking for an organization—someone, somewhere—that was trying to do something to change segregation. I heard about a series of workshops conducted by Reverend James Lawson, a conscientious objector who had spent some time in India and was extremely well versed in nonviolence. So I went to these workshops, and I listened very carefully. After a few weeks, I decided this nonviolence couldn't possibly have any impact. But because they were the only group in Nashville that was trying to make a change, I kept going. I learned that you can respect a person, and at the same time, not tolerate oppression and the actions that person is doing—that you can attack the philosophy without attacking the person.

In the fall of 1959 we started going to restaurants downtown and trying to get served. When we were refused service, we would ask to see the manager, ask him why we were being refused service, and then tell him we thought it was morally wrong. We called that testing. In February of 1960 we heard

on the radio that sit-ins had begun in other southern cities—
Greensboro, Orangeburg, Knoxville. We jumped up and down
and applauded, and then we decided to have our sit-ins at the
same chains that the students were targeting in other cities.

The Student Nonviolent Coordinating Committee Is Born

As the sit-in movement spread, the executive director of the
Southern Christian Leadership Conference, Ella Baker, decided
it would be a good idea to bring the participating students together in one place for a conference. Over the Easter weekend
in 1960 we all gathered at Shaw University in Raleigh, North
Carolina. At the conference, we discussed the need for a central place to gather and disseminate information and the value
in coordinating some of our activities on a Southwide kind of
basis. We also decided not to become the student arm of an
older organization, because we did not want to be taking orders from a distant board of directors. The Student Nonviolent Coordinating Committee was formed, and we distin-
guished ourselves from the older organizations, because in
SNCC, the people who did the work and took the chances
were the ones who made the decisions.

By 1962 I had left Fisk University to devote all my time to
the civil rights movement. In May I was in Mississippi, where
the bus system was still legally segregated, encouraging black
young people to sit at the front of the bus and conducting
workshops in nonviolence to prepare students for the filings
they needed to know in order to join in the Freedom Rides. I
was twenty-three at the time, and since I was encouraging
these minors to do something illegal, a warrant was issued for
my arrest, charging me with contributing to the delinquency
of minors. I faced a two-and-a-half-year jail term, and I was
about six months pregnant with my first child. My husband
drove me down to Jackson and I surrendered to the sheriff,
and the following Monday I surrendered to the court. I sat in

the first bench in the first row and refused to move to the rear when the bailiff ordered me to do so, so I was put in jail for ten days for contempt of court.

Jail Time

Those ten days were really hard. The jail had so many cockroaches that I soon learned to sleep during the day so that I could sit up at night and dodge them as they dropped off the ceiling onto my cot. One night there was an insect that was so large I could actually hear it walking across the floor. I had taken a toothbrush, comb, and my vitamin pills (since I was expecting), a change of underwear, and an extra skirt and blouse, because I knew I was going to jail. But the prison officials would not let me have anything, not a toothbrush, not toothpaste, nothing. I was determined not to be demoralized, so I worked out a little schedule. I had clean clothes every day because I would wash my underwear and my outerwear at different times and they could dry while I was asleep. I remember combing my hair with my fingers and working out a way to brush my teeth. I emerged from the experience even stronger because I learned that I could get along with nothing if I had to—except food and water perhaps. I never got to the point where I felt like I had to quit, because when the officials would do oppressive things, it deepened my resolve and made me angrier.

When you are faced with a situation of injustice or oppression, if you change yourself and become somebody who cannot be oppressed, then the world has to set up against a new you. We students became people who could not be segregated. They could have killed us, but they could not segregate us any longer. Once that happened, the whole country was faced with a new set of decisions. I think most of the students that were participating were confident that we could change the world. I still think we can.

Bloody Sunday: The Protest March that Shocked the Nation

John F. Lewis

When civil rights marchers crossed the Edmund Pettus Bridge in Selma, Alabama, on March 7, 1965, to demonstrate for equality in voter registration in Alabama, they came face-to-face with state troopers bent on stopping them by whatever means necessary. That fateful day came to be known as Bloody Sunday because of the viciousness of the troopers' attack on the demonstrators. What happened in Selma that day has been called the most important march of the civil rights movement because of its impact on the American public. Television and radio coverage of the attack, and the nonviolent manner in which marchers endured it, both shocked and inspired the nation.

The leader of the march, John Lewis, was a young man who had participated in many demonstrations. The son of sharecroppers, Lewis had worked with Diane Nash to organize the Nashville sit-ins, had been savagely beaten on the first Freedom Ride, had helped found the Student Nonviolent Coordinating Committee (SNCC), and had spoken at the 1963 March on Washington.

In the following excerpt from his autobiography, Walking with the Wind, *Lewis recalls Bloody Sunday in intimate detail. He tells how they prepared for the march and the sense of fear and panic he felt when they were attacked. He also vividly describes its aftermath, "awash with sounds of groaning and weeping." Today, Lewis represents the state of Georgia in the U.S. House of Representatives.*

John F. Lewis with Michael D'Orso, in *Walking With the Wind: A Memoir of the Movement*. New York: Simon & Schuster, 1998, pp. 323–31. Copyright © 1998 by John Lewis. All rights reserved. Abridged by permission of Simon & Schuster Adult Publishing Group.

It was mid-afternoon now, and time to assemble. A team of doctors and nurses from a group called the Medical Committee for Human Rights had arrived the day before on a flight from New York and set up a makeshift clinic in the small parsonage beside the church [Brown Chapel AME (African Methodist Episcopal) Church]. We expected a confrontation. We knew Sheriff [Jim] Clark had issued yet another call the evening before for even more deputies. Mass arrests would probably be made. There might be injuries. Most likely, we would be stopped at the edge of the city limits, arrested and maybe roughed up a little bit. We did not expect anything worse than that.

And we did *not* expect to march all the way to Montgomery. No one knew for sure, until the last minute, if the march would even take place. There had been a measure of planning, but nowhere near the preparations and logistics necessary to move that many people in an orderly manner down fifty-four miles of highway, a distance that would take about five days for a group that size to cover.

Many of the men and women gathered on that ballfield had come straight from church. They were still wearing their Sunday outfits. Some of the women had on high heels. I had on a suit and tie, a light tan raincoat, dress shoes and my backpack. I was no more ready to hike half a hundred miles than anyone else. Like everyone around me, I was basically playing it by ear. None of us had thought much further ahead than that afternoon. Anything that happened beyond that—if we were allowed to go on, if this march did indeed go all the way to Montgomery—we figured we would take care of as we went along. The main thing was that we *do* it, that we march.

We Set Out

It was close to 4 P.M. when Andy [Young], Hosea [Williams], [James] Bevel and I gathered the marchers around us. A dozen or so reporters were there as well. I read a short statement aloud for the benefit of the press, explaining why we were marching today. Then we all knelt to one knee and bowed our heads as Andy delivered a prayer.

And then we set out, nearly six hundred of us, including a white SCLC [Southern Christian Leadership Conference] staffer named Al Lingo—the same name as the commander of Alabama's state troopers.

We walked two abreast, in a pair of lines that stretched for several blocks. Hosea and I led the way. Albert Turner, an SCLC leader in Perry County and Bob Mants were right behind us—Bob insisted on marching because I was marching; he told me he wanted to be there to "protect" me in case something happened.

[Selma activists] Marie Foster and Amelia Boynton were next in line, and behind them, stretching as far as I could see, walked an army of teenagers, teachers, undertakers, beauticians—many of the same Selma people who had stood for weeks, months, *years*, in front of that courthouse.

At the far end, bringing up the rear, rolled four slow-moving ambulances.

Almost Like a Funeral Procession

I can't count the number of marches I have participated in in my lifetime, but there was something peculiar about this one. It was more than disciplined. It was somber and subdued, almost like a funeral procession. No one was jostling or pushing to get to the front, as often happened with these things. I don't know if there was a feeling that something was going to happen, or if the people simply sensed that this was a special procession, a "leaderless" march. There were no big names up front, no celebrities. This was just plain folks moving through the streets of Selma.

There was a little bit of a crowd looking on as we set out down the red sand of Sylvan Street, through the black section of town. There was some cheering and singing from those onlookers and from a few of the marchers, but then, as we turned right along Water Street, out of the black neighborhood now, the mood changed. There was no singing, no shouting—just the sound of scuffling feet. There was something holy about it, as if we were walking down a sacred path. It reminded me of Gandhi's march to the sea. Dr. [Martin Luther] King used to say there is nothing more powerful than the rhythm of marching feet, and that was what this was, the marching feet of a determined people. That was the only sound you could hear.

We Cross the Bridge

Down Water Street we went, turning right and walking along the river until we reached the base of the bridge, the Edmund Pettus Bridge.

There was a small posse of armed white men there, gathered in front of the *Selma Times-Journal* building. They had hard hats on their heads and clubs in their hands. Some of them were smirking. Not one said a word. I didn't think too much of them as we walked past. I'd seen men like that so many times.

As we turned onto the bridge, we were careful to stay on the narrow sidewalk. The road had been closed to traffic, but we still stayed on the walkway, which was barely wide enough for two people.

I noticed how steep it was as we climbed toward the steel canopy at the top of the arched bridge. It was too steep to see the other side. I looked down at the river and saw how still it was, still and brown. The surface of the water was stirred just a bit by the late-afternoon breeze. I noticed my trench coat was riffling a little from that same small wind.

When we reached the crest of the bridge, I stopped dead still.

So did Hosea.

There, facing us at the bottom of the other side, stood a sea of blue-helmeted, blue-uniformed Alabama state troopers, line after line of them, dozens of battle-ready lawmen stretched from one side of U.S. Highway 80 to the other.

Behind them were several dozen more armed men—Sheriff Clark's posse—some on horseback, all wearing khaki clothing, many carrying clubs the size of baseball bats.

On one side of the road I could see a crowd of about a hundred whites, laughing and hollering, waving Confederate flags. Beyond them, at a safe distance, stood a small, silent group of black people.

"Can You Swim?"

I could see a crowd of newsmen and reporters gathered in the parking lot of a Pontiac dealership. And I could see a line of parked police and state trooper vehicles. I didn't know it at the time, but Clark and [Alabama state trooper, Al] Lingo were in one of those cars.

It was a drop of one hundred feet from the top of that bridge to the river below. Hosea glanced down at the muddy water and said, "Can you swim?"

"No," I answered.

"Well," he said, with a tiny half smile, "neither can I."

"But," he added, lifting his head and looking straight ahead, "we might have to."

Then we moved forward. The only sounds were our footsteps on the bridge and the snorting of a horse ahead of us.

I noticed several troopers slipping gas masks over their faces as we approached.

At the bottom of the bridge, while we were still about fifty feet from the troopers, the officer in charge, a Major John Cloud, stepped forward, holding a small bullhorn up to his mouth.

Hosea and I stopped, which brought the others to a standstill.

"*This is an unlawful assembly,*" Cloud pronounced. "*Your march is not conducive to the public safety. You are ordered to disperse and go back to your church or to your homes.*"

"May we have a word with the major?" asked Hosea.

"*There is no word to be had,*" answered Cloud.

Hosea asked the same question again, and got the same response.

Then Cloud issued a warning: "*You have two minutes to turn around and go back to your church.*"

What Now?

I wasn't about to turn around. We were there. We were not going to run. We couldn't turn and go back even if we wanted to. There were too many people.

We could have gone forward, marching right into the teeth of those troopers. But that would have been too aggressive, I thought, too provocative. God knew what might have happened if we had done that. These people were ready to be arrested, but I didn't want anyone to get hurt.

We couldn't go forward. We couldn't go back. There was only one option left that I could see.

"We should kneel and pray," I said to Hosea.

He nodded.

We turned and passed the word back to begin bowing down in a prayerful manner.

But that word didn't get far. It didn't have time. One minute after he had issued his warning—I know this because I was careful to check my watch—Major Cloud issued an order to his troopers.

"*Troopers,*" he barked. "*Advance!*"

And then all hell broke loose.

Clubs and Tear Gas

The troopers and possemen swept forward as one, like a human wave, a blur of blue shirts and billy clubs and bullwhips. We had no chance to turn and retreat. There were six hundred people behind us, bridge railings to either side and the river below.

I remember how vivid the sounds were as the troopers rushed toward us—the clunk of the troopers' heavy boots, the whoops of rebel yells from the white onlookers, the clip-clop of horses' hooves hitting the hard asphalt of the highway, the voice of a woman shouting, "Get 'em! *Get* the niggers!"

And then they were upon us. The first of the troopers came over me, a large, husky man. Without a word, he swung his club against the left side of my head. I didn't feel any pain, just the thud of the blow, and my legs giving way. I raised an arm—a reflex motion—as I curled up in the "prayer for protection" position. And then the same trooper hit me again. And everything started to spin.

I heard something that sounded like gunshots. And then a cloud of smoke rose all around us.

Tear gas.

I'd never experienced tear gas before. This, I would learn later, was a particularly toxic form called C-4, made to induce nausea.

I began choking, coughing. I couldn't get air into my lungs. I felt as if I was taking my last breath. If there was ever a time in my life for me to panic, it should have been then. But I didn't. I remember how strangely calm I felt as I thought, This is it. People are going to die here. *I'm* going to die here.

I really felt that I saw death at that moment, that I looked it right in its face. And it felt strangely soothing. I had a feeling that it would be so easy to just lie down there, just lie down and let it take me away.

Another Viewpoint

That was the way those first few seconds looked from where I stood—and lay. Here is how Roy Reed, a reporter for *The New York Times*, described what he saw:

> The troopers rushed forward, their blue uniforms and white helmets blurring into a flying wedge as they moved.

The wedge moved with such force that it seemed almost to pass over the waiting column instead of through it.

The first 10 or 20 Negroes were swept to the ground screaming, arms and legs flying, and packs and bags went skittering across the grassy divider strip and on to the pavement on both sides.

Those still on their feet retreated.

The troopers continued pushing, using both the force of their bodies and the prodding of their nightsticks.

A cheer went up from the white spectators lining the south side of the highway.

The mounted possemen spurred their horses and rode at a run into the retreating mass. The Negroes cried out as they crowded together for protection, and the whites on the sidelines whooped and cheered.

The Negroes paused in their retreat for perhaps a minute, still screaming and huddling together.

Suddenly there was a report like a gunshot and a grey cloud spewed over the troopers and the Negroes.

"Tear gas!" someone yelled.

The cloud began covering the highway. Newsmen, who were confined by four troopers to a corner 100 yards away, began to lose sight of the action.

But before the cloud finally hid it all, there were several seconds of unobstructed view. Fifteen or twenty nightsticks could be seen through the gas, flailing at the heads of the marchers.

The Negroes broke and ran. Scores of them streamed across the parking lot of the Selma Tractor Company. Troopers and possemen, mounted and unmounted, went after them.

Chaos Around Me

I was bleeding badly. My head was now exploding with pain. That brief, sweet sense of just wanting to lie there was gone. I needed to get up. I'd faded out for I don't know how long, but now I was tuned back in.

There was mayhem all around me. I could see a young kid—a teenaged boy—sitting on the ground with a gaping cut in his head, the blood just gushing out. Several women, including Mrs. Boynton, were lying on the pavement and the grass median. People were weeping. Some were vomiting from the tear gas. Men on horses were moving in all directions, purposely riding over the top of fallen people, bringing their animals' hooves down on shoulders, stomachs and legs.

The mob of white onlookers had joined in now, jumping cameramen and reporters. One man filming the action was knocked down and his camera was taken away. The man turned out to be an FBI agent, and the three men who attacked him were later arrested. One of them was Jimmie George Robinson, the man who had attacked Dr. King at the Hotel Albert.

I was up now and moving, back across the bridge, with troopers and possemen and other retreating marchers all around me. At the other end of the bridge, we had to push through the possemen we'd passed outside the *Selma Times-Journal* building.

"Please, *no*," I could hear one woman scream.

"God, we're being *killed!*" cried another.

With nightsticks and whips—one posseman had a rubber hose wrapped with barbed wire—Sheriff Clark's "deputies" chased us all the way back into the Carver project and up to the front of Brown's Chapel, where we tried getting as many people as we could inside the church to safety. I don't even recall how I made it that far, how I got from the bridge to the church, but I did.

The Attack Continues

A United Press International reporter gave this account of that segment of the attack:

> The troopers and possemen, under Gov. George C. Wallace's orders to stop the Negroes' "Walk for Freedom" from Selma

to Montgomery, chased the screaming, bleeding marchers nearly a mile back to their church, clubbing them as they ran.

Ambulances screamed in relays between Good Samaritan Hospital and Brown's Chapel Church, carrying hysterical men, women and children suffering head wounds and tear gas burns.

Even then, the possemen and troopers, 150 of them, including Clark himself, kept attacking, beating anyone who remained on the street. Some of the marchers fought back now, with men and boys emerging from the Carver homes with bottles and bricks in their hands, heaving them at the troopers, then retreating for more. It was a scene that's been replayed so many times in so many places—in Belfast, in Jerusalem, in Beijing. Angry, desperate people hurling whatever they can at the symbols of authority, their hopeless fury much more powerful than the futile bottles and bricks in their hands.

I was inside the church, which was awash with sounds of groaning and weeping. And singing and crying. Mothers shouting out for their children. Children screaming for their mothers and brothers and sisters. So much confusion and fear and anger all erupting at the same time.

Further up Sylvan Street, the troopers chased other marchers who had fled into the First Baptist Church. A teenaged boy, struggling with the possemen, was thrown through a church window there.

Treating the Wounded

Finally [director of pubic safety] Wilson Baker arrived and persuaded Clark and his men to back off to a block away, where they remained, breathing heavily and awaiting further orders.

A crowd of Selma's black men and women had collected in front of the church by now, with SNCC and SCLC staff members moving through and trying to keep them calm. Some men in the crowd spoke of going home to get guns. Our people tried talking them down, getting them calm. Kids and teenagers continued throwing rocks and bricks.

The parsonage next to the church looked like a MASH unit, with doctors and nurses tending to dozens of weeping, wounded people. There were cuts and bumps and bruises, and a lot of tear gas burns, which were treated by rinsing the eyes with a boric acid solution.

Relays of ambulances sent by black funeral homes carried the more seriously wounded to Good Samaritan Hospital, Selma's largest black health-care facility, run by white Catholics and staffed mostly by black doctors and nurses. One of those ambulance drivers made ten trips back and forth from the church to the hospital and to nearby Burwell Infirmary, a smaller clinic. More than ninety men and women were treated at both facilities, for injuries ranging from head gashes and fractured ribs and wrists and arms and legs to broken jaws and teeth. There was one fractured skull—mine, although I didn't know it yet. . . .

The World Learns of the Attack

It was not until the next day that I learned what else had happened that evening, that just past 9:30 P.M., ABC Television cut into its Sunday night movie—a premiere broadcast of Stanley Kramer's *Judgment at Nuremberg*, a film about Nazi racism—with a special bulletin. News anchor Frank Reynolds came on-screen to tell viewers of a brutal clash that afternoon between state troopers and black protest marchers in Selma, Alabama. They then showed fifteen minutes of film footage of the attack.

The images were stunning—scene after scene of policemen on foot and on horseback beating defenseless American citizens. Many viewers thought this was somehow part of the movie. It seemed too strange, too ugly to be real. It *couldn't* be real.

But it was. At one point in the film clip, Jim Clark's voice could be heard clearly in the background: "Get those goddamned niggers!" he yelled. "And get those goddamned *white* niggers."

The American public had already seen so much of this sort of thing, countless images of beatings and dogs and cursing and hoses. But something about that day in Selma touched a nerve deeper than anything that had come before. Maybe it was the concentrated focus of the scene, the mass movement of those troopers on foot and riders on horseback rolling into and over two long lines of stoic, silent, unarmed people. This wasn't like Birmingham, where chanting and cheering and singing preceded a wild stampede and scattering. This was a face-off in the most vivid terms between a dignified, composed, completely nonviolent multitude of silent protestors and the truly malevolent force of a heavily armed, hateful battalion of troopers. The sight of them rolling over us like human tanks was something that had never been seen before.

People just couldn't believe this was happening, not in America. Women and children being attacked by armed men on horseback—it was impossible to believe.

But it had happened. And the response from across the nation to what would go down in history as Bloody Sunday was immediate.

Chronology

1948

July 26: President Harry S. Truman issues Executive Order 9981, ending segregation in the U.S. armed forces.

1954

May 17: The U.S. Supreme Court overturns "separate but equal" in *Brown v. Board of Education*, ordering an end to segregated schools.

1955

December 1: Rosa Parks refuses to give up her seat to a white man on a bus, starting the 381-day Montgomery, Alabama, bus boycott.

1957

January: The Southern Christian Leadership Conference (SCLC) is formed.

September: Arkansas governor Orval Faubus orders National Guardsmen to block integration of Little Rock Central High School, forcing President Dwight D. Eisenhower to send in federal troops.

1960

February: Sit-ins begin at Woolworth's lunch counter in Greensboro, North Carolina.

April: The Student Nonviolent Coordinating Committee (SNCC) is formed.

May: Sit-ins begin in Nashville, Tennessee.

May 6: The Civil Rights Act of 1960 is signed into law.

1961

May 4: Freedom Rides begin.

1963

April 16: Martin Luther King Jr. writes the famous "Letter from Birmingham Jail," having been arrested during demonstrations in Birmingham, Alabama.

May 2: The Children's Campaign begins in Birmingham. Violence against demonstrators by police commissioner "Bull" Connor's law enforcement officers sparks national outrage.

June 11: President John F. Kennedy makes a historic civil rights speech, promising to send wide-reaching civil rights legislation to Congress.

August 28: The March on Washington for Jobs and Freedom takes place. King delivers his "I Have a Dream" speech.

November 22: President Kennedy is assassinated in Dallas, Texas.

1964

Summer: The Mississippi Freedom Summer—an all-out effort to register blacks to vote in Mississippi—occurs. The Mississippi Freedom Democratic Party (MFDP) tries to unseat the all-white Mississippi delegation to the Democratic National Convention in Atlantic City, New Jersey. Fannie Lou Hamer's testimony before the credentials committee draws national attention.

July 2: President Lyndon B. Johnson signs the Civil Rights Act of 1964.

1965

February 21: Malcolm X is shot to death in New York.

March 7: "Bloody Sunday," a violent confrontation between protesters and police at the Edmund Pettus Bridge in Selma, Alabama, occurs.

March 15: President Johnson delivers a speech to Congress urging passage of a voting rights bill after witnessing news coverage of "Bloody Sunday."

March 21–25: The march from Selma to Montgomery, Alabama, culminates in a mass meeting on the steps of the state capitol.

August 6: The Voting Rights Act of 1965 is signed into law.

1966

October: The Black Panther Party is founded in Oakland, California.

1968

April 4: Martin Luther King is shot and killed in Memphis, Tennessee.

April 11: The Civil Rights Act of 1968 is signed into law.

For Further Research

Books

Daisy Bates, *The Long Shadow of Little Rock: A Memoir*. Fayetteville: University of Arkansas Press, 1986.

Melba Patillo Beals, *Warriors Don't Cry: A Searing Memoir of the Battle to Integrate Little Rock's Central High*. New York: Pocket Books, 1994.

Taylor Branch, *At Canaan's Edge: America in the King Years, 1965–68*. New York: Simon & Schuster, 2006.

Taylor Branch, *Parting the Waters: America in the King Years: 1954–63*. New York: Simon & Schuster, 1988.

Taylor Branch, *Pillar of Fire: America in the King Years, 1963–65*. New York: Simon & Schuster, 1998.

Stuart Burns, *To the Mountaintop: Martin Luther King Jr.'s Sacred Mission to Save America, 1955–1968*. New York: HarperCollins, 2004.

Clayborne Carson et al., eds., *The Eyes on the Prize Civil Rights Reader: Documents, Speeches, and Firsthand Accounts from the Black Freedom Struggle, 1954–1990*. New York: Penguin, 1991.

David J. Garrow, *Bearing the Cross: Martin Luther King Jr. and the Southern Christian Leadership Conference*. New York: William Morrow, 1986.

Allison Graham, *Framing the South: Hollywood, Television, and Race During the Civil Rights Struggle*. Baltimore: Johns Hopkins University Press, 2001.

David Halberstam, *The Children*. New York: Random House, 1998.

Henry Hampton and Steve Fayer, *Voices of Freedom: An Oral History of the Civil Rights Movement from the 1950s through the 1980s*. New York: Bantam, 1990.

Casey King and Linda Barrett Osborne, *Oh, Freedom: Kids Talk About the Civil Rights Movement with the People Who Made It Happen.* New York: Knopf, 1997.

Ellen Levine, *Freedom's Children: Young Civil Rights Activists Tell Their Own Stories.* New York: Puffin, 1993.

John Lewis with Michael D'Orso, *Walking with the Wind: A Memoir of the Movement.* New York: Simon & Schuster, 1998.

Andrew M. Manis, *A Fire You Can't Put Out: The Civil Rights Life of Birmingham's Reverend Fred Shuttlesworth.* Tuscaloosa: University of Alabama Press, 1999.

Diane McWhorter, *Carry Me Home: Birmingham, Alabama; The Climactic Battle of the Civil Rights Revolution.* New York: Touchstone, 2001.

Jon Meacham, *Voices in Our Blood: America's Best on the Civil Rights Movement.* New York: Random House, 2003.

Milton Meltzer, *The Black Americans: A History in Their Own Words, 1619–1983.* New York: HarperCollins, 1984.

Kay Mills, *This Little Light of Mine: The Life of Fannie Lou Hamer.* New York: Penguin, 1993.

Lynne Olson, *Freedom's Daughters: The Unsung Heroines of the Civil Rights Movement from 1830 to 1970.* New York: Scribner, 2001.

Rosa Parks with Jim Haskins, *Rosa Parks: My Story.* New York: Puffin, 1992.

Sheyann Webb and Rachel West Nelson, *Selma, Lord, Selma: Childhood Memories of the Civil-Rights Days As Told to Frank Sikora.* Tuscaloosa: University of Alabama Press, 1980.

Andrew Young, *An Easy Burden: The Civil Rights Movement and the Transformation of America.* New York: HarperCollins, 1996.

Howard Zinn and Anthony Arnove, *Voices of a People's History of the United States*. New York: Seven Stories, 2004.

Web Sites:

African American Odyssey: The Civil Rights Era (http:// memory.loc.gov/ammem/aaohtml/exhibit/aopart9.html). Established by the Library of Congress, this Web site is part of a collection of exhibits telling the story of African American history from slavery to the civil rights era. It includes primary documents, pictures, videos, and audios from the period.

Civil Rights Movement Veterans—CORE, NAACP, SCLC, SNCC (www.crmvet.org). This Web site was written by and for veterans of the American civil rights movement. It contains pictures, oral histories, and a timeline of the movement in the South in the 1960s.

Little Rock Central High 40th Anniversary (www.centralhigh 57.org). This Web site commemorates the anniversary in 1997 of the integration of Little Rock's Central High School, including information about the Little Rock Nine; reprints of 1957 editions of the *Tiger*, Central High School's newspaper; and a virtual tour of some areas of the school.

Voices of Civil Rights: Ordinary People, Extraordinary Stories (www.voicesofcivilrights.org/project.html). This project of the American Association of Retired Persons (AARP), the Leadership Conference on Civil Rights (LCCR), and the Library of Congress, offers a collection of thousands of personal stories and oral histories of the civil rights movement, forming the world's largest archive of personal accounts of civil rights history.

Index